"Symbolism and symbolisation are central concerns in the disciplines of sociology, ethnology, and psychoanalysis, but few attempts have been made to synthesize the approaches from these different but related fields. Éric Smadja, who is both a psychoanalyst and an anthropologist, has now done so in an admirably concise but thorough treatment of the place of symbolism in the work of Durkheim, Mauss, and Freud, with further thoughts on subsequent thinkers including Levi-Strauss, Bourdieu, Lacan and others. This book will be a valuable resource for scholars seeking a lucid and systematic interdisciplinary treatment of symbolism and its key role in the mind and in sociocultural life."

Robert A. Paul, *Charles Howard Candler Professor of Anthropology and Interdisciplinary Studies, Emory University; Director, Emory University Psychoanalytic Institute, USA*

ON SYMBOLISM AND SYMBOLISATION

In *On Symbolism and Symbolisation: The Work of Freud, Durkheim and Mauss*, Éric Smadja returns to the end of the 19th century and explores how the concepts of symbolism and symbolisation have been discussed among theorists, and how this discussion has developed and revolutionised the human sciences as we know them today. Uniquely, he connects three key thinkers of psychoanalysis, sociology and ethnology – Freud, Durkheim and Mauss – and discusses how their diverse epistemological paths blend, and have consequently shaped our representation of humanity, society and culture in the 20th and 21st centuries.

In this innovative work, Smadja provides a complete biographical journey of these three influential founders, beginning with a dedicated chapter on Freud, followed by Durkheim and then Mauss. He explains each of their revolutionary creations – Freud's psychoanalysis, Durkheim's French school of sociology and Mauss's modern French ethnology – before exploring their ground-breaking, yet differing, conceptions of symbolism and symbolisation, offering a discussion of specific and common aspects detected between these conceptions. In his conclusions, Smadja focusses on France to examine what became of their thoughts after the second half of the 20th century. He inspects the fields of French anthropology, sociology and psychoanalysis: Lévi-Strauss and his structuralist revolution, his colleagues Françoise Héritier and Maurice Godelier, Pierre Bourdieu, who was an ethnologist before becoming a sociologist, and, of course, Lacan.

On Symbolism and Symbolisation: The Work of Freud, Durkheim and Mauss is a pioneering work that will appeal to psychoanalysts in practice and in training, and to academics and students of psychology, anthropology, sociology, philosophy and the history of ideas. It will also be of interest to anyone wanting to learn more about the life and work of these three major theorists and the connections between the human and social sciences.

Éric Smadja is a psychiatrist and a psychoanalyst based in Paris, France, and London, UK. He is a member of the Société Psychanalytique de Paris, a guest member of the British Psychoanalytical Society and a member of the International Psychoanalytical Association (IPA). He is also an anthropologist and an associate member of the American Anthropological Association. He was awarded the IPA's Prize for 'Exceptional Contribution Made to Psychoanalytical Research' (2007). He is the author of several books which have been translated into many languages, including *The Couple: A Pluridisciplinary Story* and *The Oedipus Complex* (both Routledge).

ON SYMBOLISM AND SYMBOLISATION

The Work of Freud, Durkheim and Mauss

Éric Smadja

LONDON AND NEW YORK

First published 2019
by Routledge
2 Park Square, Milton Park, Abingdon, Oxon OX14 4RN

and by Routledge
711 Third Avenue, New York, NY 10017

Routledge is an imprint of the Taylor & Francis Group, an informa business

© 2019 Éric Smadja

The right of Éric Smadja to be identified as author of this work has been
asserted by him in accordance with sections 77 and 78 of the Copyright,
Designs and Patents Act 1988.

All rights reserved. No part of this book may be reprinted or reproduced or
utilised in any form or by any electronic, mechanical, or other means, now
known or hereafter invented, including photocopying and recording, or in
any information storage or retrieval system, without permission in writing
from the publishers.

Trademark notice: Product or corporate names may be trademarks or
registered trademarks, and are used only for identification and explanation
without intent to infringe.

British Library Cataloguing-in-Publication Data
A catalogue record for this book is available from the British Library

Library of Congress Cataloging-in-Publication Data
Names: Smadja, Éric, author.
Title: On symbolism and symbolisation: the work of Freud, Durkheim and
Mauss/Éric Smadja.
Description: 1 Edition. | New York: Routledge, NY 2019. |
Includes bibliographical references.
Identifiers: LCCN 2018024250 (print) | LCCN 2018035417 (ebook) |
ISBN 9781351124843 (Master Ebook) | ISBN 9780815357193 (hardback) |
ISBN 9780815357209 (paperbook)
Subjects: LCSH: Signs and symbols. | Symbolism. | Freud, Sigmund,
1856–1939. | Durkheim, Émile, 1858–1917. | Mauss, Marcel, 1872–1950.
Classification: LCC BF1623.S9 (ebook) | LCC BF1623.S9 .S63 2019 (print) |
DDC 150.19/52–dc23
LC record available at https://lccn.loc.gov/2018024250

ISBN: 978-0-8153-5719-3 (hbk)
ISBN: 978-0-8153-5720-9 (pbk)
ISBN: 978-1-351-12484-3 (ebk)

Typeset in Bembo
by Deanta Global Publishing Services, Chennai, India

CONTENTS

By way of introduction   **1**
The diverse sources of symbolism   2
Notes   4

1   **Freud**   **6**
Biographical journey   6
His creation: psychoanalysis   16
Notes   22

2   **Durkheim**   **23**
Biographical journey   23
His creation: the French school of sociology   28
Notes   39

3   **Mauss**   **42**
Bibliographical journey   42
His creation: transforming–developing Durkheimian sociology   50
The creation of modern French ethnology   53
Notes   58

4   **Symbols, symbolism and symbolisation**   **60**
Durkheim, symbolism and symbolisation   60
Mauss, symbolism and symbolisation   68
Freud, symbolism and symbolisation   78
Elements for discussion   90
Notes   96

viii Contents

By way of conclusion 99

Lévi-Strauss and his structuralist revolution 100
Françoise Héritier and the body as the founding substrate of the
original categories of symbolic thought: the identical and the different 103
Maurice Godelier's critique 104
Pierre Bourdieu, symbolic power and violence 105
Lacan and the symbolic function 106
Notes 108

Bibliography 111
Index 115

BY WAY OF INTRODUCTION

This theme of symbolism and symbolisation, which made its appearance at the end of the 19th century and the beginning of the 20th century, would revolutionise all the human and social sciences all throughout the 20th century, both within each of them – thus reorganizing the diverse aspects of their own epistemological fields in different manners – and in their interrelationships.

Since the 19th century, the human sciences figuring among the sciences of the mind and grounded in interpretation – understanding, in keeping with Wilhelm Dilthey's ideas, had, in fact, been pervaded and animated by an essential split between, as Bruno Karsenti has expressed it,[1] studying human beings from the outside by analysing their social forms of existence and studying them from the inside by focussing on the individual ego, conceived of as an inwardly turned entity. This split between the collective and the individual principally translates into the division instituted between sociology and psychology, in which Émile Durkheim vigorously participated.

However, the theme of symbolism and symbolisation would become a "phenomenon of transition", a mediation-juncture between the individual and collective fields, psychology and sociology, thus acquiring a privileged status deriving from the fact that the phenomena falling into this category undermine the principle of the duality between interiority and exteriority. It would thus contribute to eliminating the split between them, then to unifying them practically and theoretically within a new epistemological space.

Nevertheless, detectable in the recent history of these human sciences are two quite distinct "epistemological" paths converging towards this common theme. It is a matter, on the one hand, of the path taken by Sigmund Freud and psychoanalysis and, on the other hand, of the one taken by Durkheim, then Marcel Mauss – the French school of sociology, then modern French ethnology – which we will examine in this work.

2 By way of introduction

Symbolism and symbolisation would then become central concepts of the human sciences which would transform the representation and understanding of human beings, societies and their cultures. However, they prompt us all the same to inquire into their diverse sources detectable in recent history.

The diverse sources of symbolism

In *L'homme total*, Karsenti (1997) observed that, as it came down to Durkheim and Durkheimians, the term "symbol" is laden with connotations inherited from the history of religions and the history of law. Indeed, he reminds us that from the beginning of the 19th century, emphasis had been placed upon religious symbolism, as instigated by Friedrich Creuzer's work *Symbolik und Mythologie der alten Völker, besonders der Griechen* (*Symbolism and Mythology of the Ancient Peoples, Especially the Greeks*) (1810–1812),[2] which had a great impact on philosophical thought – on that of G. W. F. Hegel, for example. And this juridico-religious conception greatly conditioned the way in which Durkheim would use the term "symbol" to his own ends, while in Mauss, this notion of symbolism would abandon the religious space to equip itself with *considerations of linguistic and psychological origin characteristic of a psychic function, both individual and collective*, which the religious and juridical practices would but bring up to date.

Moreover, symbolism became a *primordial object* which forced itself upon psychologists at the beginning of the 1920s. It originated in the specific domain of neuropsychology, and more precisely in the study of the psychological determination of speech disorders, in which the English psychologist Henry Head (1861–1940) played a preeminent role. Pursuing the thought of Henry Jackson (1834–1911), he was in regular contact with Mauss.

The striking feature of Head's theory, Karsenti has explained, lies in the fact that it aims to account for aphasia by the deficiency of precisely what is called symbolic expression,[3] something which reveals the fundamental interdependence of all of the behavioural dimensions and not the existence of autonomous, separate faculties and centres. So, it is by means of this human function of symbolic expression that the face of the human subject in this way recaptures its unity, conceived of as *symbolic unity*.[4] Head would also introduce the notion of *symbolic function*, producer of meaning, which would be taken up again by Mauss, then by Lévi-Strauss, who would identify it with the unconscious.

On the subject of aphasia, Freud had admittedly already revealed in his 1891 work the *systemic* and non-sectorial nature of speech disorders, in opposition to the established conceptions of his time, in particular the dominant view defended by Wernicke.

What about the psychoanalytical sources of symbolism?

Besides Freud's discovery of the symbolic nature of psychoneurotic symptoms, conferring upon them a meaning that is hidden because disguised – something which his fellow physicians had overlooked – the years from 1906 to 1920 were a time of the flowering of the notion of symbolism, understood

By way of introduction **3**

by the young psychoanalytical movement as one of the cultural expressions of the unconscious and grounded in a repressed sexual desire. Indeed, with the exception of Wilhelm Stekel's work *Sex and Dreams: The Language of Dreams* (1911),[5] other colleagues took an interest in and published on this theme using dreams, myths and other literary material. Let me first of all mention some texts by Otto Rank: *The Myth of the Birth of the Hero* (1909),[6] *Die Lohengrinsage (The Lohengrin Saga)* (1911),[7] *The Incest Theme in Literature and Legend* (1912);[8] by Karl Abraham: "Dreams and Myths" (1909);[9] by Carl Gustav Jung: *Psychology of the Unconscious: A Study of the Transformations and Symbolisms of Libido, a Contribution to the History of the Evolution of Thought* (1912);[10] and also those of Ernest Jones: *On the Nightmare* (1912),[11] "The Symbolic Significance of Salt in Folklore and Superstition" (1912),[12] "The Madonna's Conception through the Ear" (1914)[13] and "The Theory of Symbolism" (1916).[14] Moreover, in *The Significance of Psychoanalysis for the Humanities* (1913),[15] Otto Rank and Hanns Sachs outlined a programme of psychoanalysis expanded to the human sciences after having recalled the essential points of Freudian theory and presented the unconscious and its sociocultural and intrapsychic-individual forms of expression, as well as the role played by infantile sexuality. A fundamental place was accorded to symbolism and to the multiple forms of symbolisation, something which would be taken up again by Freud in the special section added to the fourth edition of *The Interpretation of Dreams* (1914).

So, when it comes to a psychological approach, would psychoanalysts be ahead of psychologists and sociologists?

Freud also discussed the symbolic of language as an innate thought disposition deriving from an *archaic legacy*, as well as the existence of a connection between the collective and individual symbolic fields correlative to an activity of unconscious representation at work in both the individual and in all of society.

Nevertheless, Karsenti points out the interest that certain areas of philosophy have in this question of symbolism, notably the philosophy of knowledge in Germany, with Ernst Cassirer's *The Philosophy of Symbolic Forms* (1923–1925–1929),[16] and the philosophy of logic and language in England, with the work of C. K. Ogden and I. A. Richards, *The Meaning of Meaning: A Study of the Influence of Language upon Thought and of the Science of Symbolism* (1923).[17]

Moreover, in his work *Le symbolique et le sacré* (2008),[18] the sociologist Camille Tarot distinguished among three families of theories of symbols and two systems of functioning.

The theories of realities–symbols conceive of symbols as powerful images giving the presence of the real. The shorter the distance between the image and the thing, the more powerful the symbol is through the impact of the real. The particularity of the image–symbol and its forcefulness is that it is the presentification of the thing.[19]

While semiotic conceptions think of the symbol in terms of signs and systems of signs and within the language in which signs seek the model of their functioning, Tarot considers that the difference between the image–symbol presentifying

4 By way of introduction

reality and the semiotic conception which makes the symbolic in the structuralist sense lies in the fact that the former is not experienced as arbitrary and is therefore non-substitutable, while the latter is arbitrary and therefore substitutable within a system. In the former, the part is the whole, while in the other the part is nothing without the whole. This difference indicates two quite distinct systems of the functioning of the human mind and of the belief which finds expression in the contrast between metonymy and metaphor.[20]

Finally, the pragmatic conceptions refer to the approaches to symbols through practices, usages, manipulations and exegeses.

Before entering into the exploration of the conceptions of symbolism and symbolisation of our three experts on the subject, which will be followed by a fruitful and necessary discussion, I have chosen to devote a chapter to each one of them, beginning with Freud, followed by Durkheim, then Mauss. Each chapter will consist of an account of the *founder*'s biographical journey and a presentation of his revolutionary creation, situated within its historical and sociocultural context.

My account of the conceptions of symbolism and symbolisation will be backed up by French specialists on both these thinkers and this theme. My discussion will identify divergences and convergences likely to lead to considerations of a more general nature – epistemological and methodological ones in particular, but also to issues of ideology and identity; one side is of all knowledge, while the other side of it is scientific.

But, it is now time to discover, or rediscover, these major players who revolutionised the social and human sciences starting at the end of the 19th century and the very beginning of the 20th century.

Notes

1 Bruno Karsenti, *L'homme total*, Paris, Presses Universitaires de France, 1997, pp. 19–20.
2 Friedrich Creuzer, *Symbolik und Mythologie der alten Völker, besonders der Griechen*, Leipzig, Karl Wilhelm Leske, 1810–1812.
3 *Op. cit.*, Karsenti, 194.
4 *Ibid.*, 196.
5 Wilhelm Stekel, *Sex and Dreams: The Language of Dreams*, Boston, The Gorham Press, 1922 (1911).
6 Otto Rank, *The Myth of the Birth of the Hero*, Baltimore MD, Johns Hopkins, 2004 (1909).
7 Otto Rank, *Die Lohengrinsage. Ein Beitrag zu ihrer Motivgestaltung und Deutung*, Deuticke, Leipzig, 1911.
8 Otto Rank, *The Incest Theme in Literature and Legend*, Baltimore MD, Johns Hopkins Press, 1991 (1912).
9 Karl Abraham, "Dreams and Myths: A Study in Folk-Psychology", *Clinical Papers and Essays on Psycho-Analysis*, London, The Hogarth Press and the Institute of Psychoanalysis, 1955, pp. 153–210.
10 Carl Gustav Jung, *Psychology of the Unconscious: A Study of the Transformations and Symbolisms of the Libido, a Contribution to the History of the Evolution of Thought*, London,

By way of introduction **5**

Kegan Paul Trench Trubner, 1916 (1912). Revised in 1952 as *Symbols of Transformation*, published in his Collected Works, vol. 5.

11 Ernest Jones, *On the Nightmare*, London, The Hogarth Press, 1931.

12 Ernest Jones, "The Symbolic Significance of Salt in Folklore and Superstition", *Salt and the Alchemical Soul*, Stanton Marlan (ed.), Woodstock CT, Spring Publications, 1995, pp. 47–100.

13 Ernest Jones, "The Madonna's Conception through the Ear: A Contribution to the Relationship between Aesthetics and Religion", in Ernest Jones, *Essays in Applied Psycho-Analysis*, London, Hogarth Press, 1951, vol. 2, pp. 266–357.

14 Ernest Jones, "The Theory of Symbolism", *British Journal of Psychology* 9, 181–239.

15 Otto Rank and Hanns Sachs, "The Significance of Psychoanalysis for the Humanities", *The American Imago, a Psychoanalytic Journal for the Arts and Sciences* 22, 1964 (1913), pp. 6–133.

16 Ernst Cassirer, *Philosophy of Symbolic Forms*, New Haven CT, Yale University Press, 1955–1957 (1923–1929).

17 C. K. Ogden, and I. A. Richards, *The Meaning of Meaning: A Study of the Influence of Language upon Thought and of the Science of Symbolism*, 10th ed. With supplementary essays by Bronislaw Malinowski and F. G. Crookshank, London, Routledge & Kegan Paul, 1949 (1923).

18 Camille Tarot, *Le symbolique et le sacré: théories de la religion*, Paris, La Découverte, 2008.

19 *Ibid.*, p. 85.

20 *Ibid.*, p. 87.

1

FREUD

Biographical journey

Inspired by *Sigmund Freud: Life and Work* by Ernest Jones.[1]
Sigmund Freud was born in Freiberg, Moravia, on May 6, 1856.

Family

His father, Jakob Freud, had been born in Tysmenitz, in Galicia, on December 18, 1815 and died on October 23, 1896. He was a wool merchant and married twice, the first time at 17; two sons were born of his first marriage. They were Emmanuel, born in 1832, and Philipp, born in 1836. Widowed at the age of 40, he married Amalia Nathansohn on July 29, 1855 in Vienna. By that time, Jakob Freud was already a grandfather, and his more than 20-year-old son already had a 1-year-old son himself.

Sigmund's mother came from Brody, a town located northeast of Galicia, near the Russian border. Her parents moved to Vienna when she was still a child. Less than 20 years old at the time of her marriage, at the age of 21, she gave to birth to her first child, Sigmund, followed by five daughters and two sons: Julius, who died at the age of 8 months; Anna, two-and-a-half years younger than Freud; Rosa, Marie, Adolfine, Paula and Alexander, who was ten years younger than Sigmund. They all married except Adolfine, who remained with her mother.

Freiberg (Pribor in Czech) was a peaceful little town located in southeast Moravia. Czech was the language most used, but among themselves Jews spoke German or Yiddish. Economic hard times combined with Czech nationalism, which increasingly rejected Jews, made the Freud family decide to leave Freiberg in October 1859 for Vienna via Leipzig, while Emmanuel, his wife and their two children, as well as his brother Philipp, left for Manchester, England.

Childhood and adolescence

Sigmund was 3 years old when he arrived in Vienna with his family, who settled down in Leopoldstadt, a neighbourhood principally inhabited by Jews. His first years in his new home were difficult. He already missed country pleasures which he would only come to know again thirteen years later.

At the age of 9, Freud took an exam allowing him to enter Sperl Gymnasium a year early. Particularly studious, reading and schoolwork took up most of his time, which enabled him to remain at the head of his class for several years. From the age of 13, he often accompanied his father on his excursions in the area surrounding Vienna. Hiking, notably in the mountains, was his principal sport and source of physical exercise and would remain so for his whole life.

Almost nothing is known of his religious education. His father had very obviously been raised in the Jewish tradition, which he imparted to his son. However, although Sigmund grew up without any religious belief, he felt Jewish all the same and did little to befriend non-Jews. He must have suffered a great deal at school, and even more at university, from the anti-Semitism rampant in Vienna.

At the age of 17, he passed his exams with an honourable mention. He had not come to any decision about the choice of a profession, and his father left him entirely free. It must be pointed out that the only careers open to Viennese Jews were in industry or business, law and medicine. Freud's intellectual mind easily made him disinclined to pursue the two first professions, while he was not particularly attracted to medicine. He was curious about both nature and its enigmas and humanity and its origins. Moreover, as he was very steeped in the belief in science which peaked during the 1870s and 1880s and was strongly attracted to Darwinian theory, then in vogue, as well as to Goethe's essay on *Nature*, he finally decided to enrol in medical school.

Medical studies

He was only 17 years old when he entered the Vienna medical school in the fall of 1873. There he took courses in zoology, botany, anatomy, mineralogy and anatomical dissection, alongside which he attended philosophy courses taught by Franz Brentano, a Catholic priest, who was also the teacher of the father of phenomenology, Edmund Husserl. At the end of his third year of university, in 1876, he was admitted to the Viennese Physiological Institute of the German scientist Ernst Brücke as *famulus*, that is, as a research assistant. This Institute pursued the ideas of Hermann Helmholtz' school, in which physico-chemical forces were at work in the organism.

Brücke, who had a particularly strong and lasting influence on Freud, an object of veneration, was assisted by Ernst von Fleischl-Marxow and Sigmund Exner. From the time he arrived, he asked Freud to study the histology, inchoate up to that point, of the nerve cells of the spinal ganglia and spinal cord of a fish

8 Freud

called Petromyzon. Through his early work, Freud contributed to opening the way to the theory of neurons, having very early and very clearly detected the physiological and morphological uniqueness of nerve cells. But unlike Waldeyer, who is generally credited with the definitive creation of the theory of neurons (1891), Freud would not carry his research out to its logical conclusion.

The only lectures which really interested him during his university years were those of Meynert on psychiatry. He was granted his medical degree on March 31, 1881, and then continued to work at Brücke's Institute; he was appointed assistant at that time for fifteen months, until July 1882. However, owing to his serious material difficulties and those of his father, who had helped him financially during all those years, Brücke strongly advised him to abandon his laboratory work in order to practice medicine, all the more so because the laboratory offered no future prospects. It was quite painful for him to give up physiology at that time.

Besides, a happy event occurred to hasten things. Shortly before, Freud had met Martha Bernays from Hamburg, with whom he fell in love. They celebrated their engagement on June 17, 1882.

Then, on July 31, he went to work at Vienna General Hospital. In fact, to earn his living by practicing medicine, he absolutely had to acquire some clinical knowledge, both medical and surgical, at the hospital, which was something he totally lacked. Circumstances therefore obliged him to remain there for three whole years. He worked in particular in the psychiatric ward of Meynert, considered to be the greatest brain anatomist, where he was immediately appointed medical intern. He obtained Meynert's authorisation to work in his laboratory and spent two years there, until the summer of 1885. Inclined towards microscopy, Freud proposed that Meynert's assistant Holländer work with him on the in-depth study of the brain of new-born babies. He was already attracted to neurology and asked the opinion of his friend Breuer, whom he met at Brücke's Institute, about his orientation towards this specialty, of which the latter would approve. He then applied for a post in the ward of nervous illnesses and, in the meantime, in that of syphilitics.

Helped by different colleagues, Freud tried his hand at various kinds of research involving electric treatments, which were very much in favour in neurology at the time, but also engaged in research devoted to cocaine, which he would complete on June 18, 1884. He in fact considered cocaine to be an analgesic and not an anaesthetic, and was on the whole much more interested in its internal use than in any of its external applications. It was the ophthalmologist Koller who discovered its anaesthetic properties and published a paper on this in September 1884.

The year 1885 was a happy one for Freud. Besides his being named *Privat Dozent*, he obtained a grant enabling him to go to Charcot's neurology clinic in Paris for nineteen weeks, from October 13, 1885 to February 28, 1886. La Salpétrière hospital was the Mecca of neurologists, and Charcot was at the height of his fame. Freud had obtained a letter of introduction to him from

Benedikt, the Viennese hypnotist. What most impressed Freud about Charcot's teaching were his revolutionary views about hysteria. In this way, he awakened in Freud a strong attraction to psychopathology.

Before his departure, the paediatrician Max Kassowitz offered him a position as the director of a new neurology ward which had just been inaugurated in the first public paediatric institute, a position Freud would occupy for several years.

At the end of February 1886, Freud left Paris to spend some weeks in Berlin so as to acquire deeper knowledge of childhood illnesses from Adolf Baginski.

As a neurologist in private practice

Upon his return, starting in April 1886, Freud began practicing as a neurologist and building up a private clientele principally composed of neurotics. During this same year, after a long engagement, he married Martha on September 13 at the City Hall in Wandsbeck, Germany. She had just turned 25, and he was 30. They would have six children. The first three, Mathilde (October 16, 1887), Jean-Martin (December 7, 1889) and Oliver (February 19, 1891) were born in their first flat. Then, the Freud family moved to 19 Berggasse in August 1891, where the three other children were born one after the other: Ernst (April 6, 1892), Sophie (April 12, 1893) and Anna (December 3, 1895).

The therapeutic question then became urgent. Freud began by applying orthodox electric treatment as described by Erb, but Charcot's reticence contributed to bringing him to abandon it fairly quickly, although he was also familiar with Breuer's cathartic method. However, he used electric treatment for several months, accompanied by diverse adjuvants such as baths and massage. But, in December 1887, he turned to hypnotic suggestion and continued to use it for the next eighteen months. This method often met with encouraging success. Charcot used it, but most physicians and psychiatrists thought of it as mystification or even worse. Meynert was fiercely opposed to it, considering it degrading to the patient's dignity. Nevertheless, Freud found that his hypnoses were not always successful. So, in view of perfecting his technique, in the summer of 1889 he travelled to Nancy to meet with Liebault and Bernheim, representatives of this school opposed to that of the hospital of La Salpêtrière.

Although he had little liking for clinical neurology, he was keenly interested in clinical psychopathology, which he sensed would become a way of approaching general psychology, even the best way. His ideas brought him increasingly into conflict with his respectful colleagues and mentors, notably with regard to his serious approach to hysteria, in men in particular, but also with regard to the importance accorded to trauma, his interest in hypnosis and, later, his assessment of the role of sexual factors in neurotics (1895). Within this difficult context, he sought support from colleagues enjoying well-established, recognized positions, like Josef Breuer, who had made significant discoveries and had not hesitated to use hypnosis. So, between 1885 and 1890, and even more so between 1890

10 Freud

and 1895, Freud attempted to reawaken in Breuer that interest which problems of hysteria had inspired in him and to encourage him to make the case of Anna O. known.

I shall return to this at a later point.

During these years, Freud published his first book, *On Aphasia* (1891), which was dedicated to Breuer and was subtitled *A Critical Study* – a well-justified qualification, because it essentially contained a radical, revolutionary critique of the nearly unanimously accepted theory of aphasia defended by Wernicke-Lichtheim. And Freud was the first to make similar criticisms. This book was not very successful, despite the later recognition of its conclusions. Between 1891 and 1893, he also published articles on infantile paralysis, which brought him renown in this domain.

Between 1889 and 1892, familiar with the cathartic method, Freud observed that many patients rebelled against hypnosis. That was the first reason that led him to look for methods that did not depend on patients' aptitude to hypnotism. He would discover others, among them the dissimulation of resistance phenomena and transference, essential characteristics of psychoanalytical theory and practice. That was certainly his main reason for abandoning hypnosis and going from Breuer's cathartic method to the method of free association, which became the "psychoanalytical" method and evolved little by little between 1892 and 1896, becoming purified and ridding itself more and more of the adjuvants – hypnosis, suggestion, pressure – which had accompanied its beginnings. All that would be left of hypnosis was the couch.

But let us go back to the collaboration with Breuer. Despite some resistance, Breuer accepted, and together they published in January 1893 "The Psychical Mechanism of Hysterical Phenomena", which still retains a historical value. Breuer already recognised the importance of transference. Then, in "The Neuro-Psychoses of Defence" (1894), Freud brought up the importance of sexual troubles in their aetiology for the first time.

Studies on Hysteria, a work published in 1895, is considered as marking the beginning of psychoanalysis. Much of it was written around the middle of 1894. It was unfortunately rather poorly received in medical milieu but, however, aroused attention in other circles.

The two men's views on the theory of hysteria soon diverged. They ceased collaborating during the summer of 1894, as Breuer was unable to accept the idea that sexuality troubles could be the essential factor in the aetiology of both neuroses and psychoses. Freud would then complain of his isolation following this painful split. Nevertheless, Wilhelm Fliess would become a good successor. He was a Berlin physician who specialised in afflictions of the nose and throat with whom Freud began a regular correspondence in 1893, which they pursued until September 1902.

What he asked of Fliess above all was that he familiarise himself with Freud's latest discoveries and the theoretical explanations he was drawing from them, and then to judge them. Fliess played an even more important role by quietly sanctioning ideas whose publication he authorised, and that was what Freud needed. Upon his return from a short stay in Berlin where he met Fliess and had a nose operation, Freud wrote enthusiastically, and only for his friend, his *Project for a Scientific Psychology* which, incidentally, he left untitled. He sent this manuscript with his letter of October 8, 1895. In this essay, he used the terminology of physics and brain physiology. In his introduction, he explained that the goal of this essay was to make psychology a natural science. Among the *Project*'s major contributions may be mentioned, in particular, the existence of two categories of psychic processes: the primary process, aiming at pure discharge of excitation, and the secondary process which, beginning with attention, extends from perception to thought processes.

It was in an article written in French and published on March 30, 1896 that the word "psychoanalysis" figured for the first time; it appeared in German on May 15, 1896.

The death of Freud's father in October 1896 was the event that led him to undertake his self-analysis, beginning in the summer of 1897, as well as to write *The Interpretation of Dreams*. His interest in the interpretation of dreams had two points of departure. By studying the ever freer associations of his patients, he observed that they often inserted the story of some dream with its associations. Then, his psychiatric experience of hallucinatory states in psychotics often enabled him to see an obvious wish-fulfilment in these states. In addition, long suspecting that dreams essentially consisted of the fulfilment of a hidden desire, he found this confirmed by the first complete analysis of the dream of *Irma's injection* (July 24, 1895).

Completed in September 1899, *Die Traumdeutung* went on sale on November 4, 1899, but its publisher, Deuticke, nevertheless preferred to date it 1900. "Freud's book," observed Anzieu,

> is both the account and the result of the self-analysis which enabled him to isolate himself from the rest of the world for a little over four years, from July 1895 to September 1899, and to reconstruct his own internal reality mainly with Fliess's help.[2]

Anzieu considered this publication the first book of psychoanalysis and that it contained the programme for Freud's later writings and those of his successors. It potentially contains such a considerable number of ideas and facts that they have yet to be completely investigated. Unfortunately, the book did not meet with the abundant and frank success hoped for. Reviews were rare, superficial and even nasty. It did not sell, and the publisher complained about this. Freud's professional and scientific isolation was at its height. He was hoping for fame and a resultant influx of clientele. But it was the other way around, leaving him still in penury and with the spectre of poverty. Patients who were cured went away, and new patients did not stay on.

12 Freud

The years 1900–1910

This first decade of the century was certainly the happiest of Freud's life. Apart from the setting in of the break with Fliess between March 1901 and March 1902, Freud finally made his first trip to Rome in September 1901. For Anzieu, the change of attitude ushered in by the trip to Rome was for Freud the major personal benefit of self-analysis, which was,

> of course, very fertile from a scientific point of view. Up to then, he had been guided by a selfish ambition to become great scientist, and was always ready to react intransigently and scornfully to those who questioned his discoveries. We now find someone more concerned with practical efficiency, ready to take the concrete human realities into account, and soon to turn his energies to the social organisation of psychoanalysis, its dissemination, its applications, and the training of its practitioners.[3]

In 1902, after encountering multiple obstacles and with the support of some people, among them his ex-colleague Exner, he was finally appointed assistant professor. He at least became respected, which coincided with the gradual end of his intellectual isolation, which had lasted, according to him, around ten years. Every Saturday he gave a weekly lecture at the university on the psychology of neuroses, which he would continue doing for three years. His private clientele had distinctly grown and occupied most of his time. Few of his patients came from Vienna. Most of them were from eastern Europe – Russia, Hungary, Poland and Rumania, in particular.

Beginning that same year and, regularly from then on, a certain number of young physicians gathered around him to learn psychoanalysis. Among those attending his lectures were two physicians, Max Kahane and Rudolf Reitler, the latter being the first, after Freud, to practice psychoanalysis. Kahane proposed that Wilhelm Stekel meet Freud, with whom Stekel then underwent analysis. During the fall of 1902, upon Stekel's suggestion, Freud proposed that Kahane, Reitler, Stekel and Adler meet with him to discuss his work, thus founding the first society of psychoanalysis – called the "Wednesday Psychological Society", because they met every Wednesday evening to discuss in Freud's waiting room. After the spring of 1908, it would be established as the "Vienna Psychoanalytic Society".

Over the course of the next few years, other colleagues joined this group, among them: Federn (1903), then Hitschmann (1905), introduced by Federn; Rank (1906), introduced by Adler; then Sadger (1906), Ferenczi (1908), Tausk (1909), Sachs and Silberer (1910). Then invited guests showed up, among them: Eitingon (January 1902), Jung and Binswanger (March 1907), Abraham (December 1907) and Brill and Jones (May 1908).

If Freud's writings had been ignored by German journals of neurology and psychology for several years, or accompanied by contemptuous commentaries, in

English-speaking countries, certain periodicals proved to be more well disposed and kindly, without nevertheless being too quick to accept these new ideas.

Moreover, during the fall of 1904, Eugen Bleuler, a professor of psychiatry from Zurich, announced to Freud that he and his whole team had for several years taken a lively interest in psychoanalysis; they had even began to study and discover some applications for it. Furthermore, it was Carl Gustav Jung, Bleuler's principal assistant, who suggested undertaking this work. Jung had in fact read *The Interpretation of Dreams* very early on and mentioned it in his work on the occult, published in 1902. As early as 1904, he had applied Freud's ideas in diverse domains, among them psychoses. Then, in April 1906, the two began to correspond, and would do so for around seven years, during which an intense friendship was built up. In addition, the "Freud Society" was founded in Zurich in 1907, composed of Jung, the leader, Bleuler, Riklin, Maeder and all of Zurich.

Freud considered psychoanalysis then to begin expanding extraordinarily rapidly during these years, following the establishment of relations between the schools of Vienna and Zurich, that is, beginning in 1907. So, in April 1908 Jung organised an initial general meeting of all those interested in Freud's works called the "Meeting of Freudian Psychologists" that gathered his first disciples, among them Abraham, Ferenczi, Jones, Jung and the Viennese. Freud presented there the case of an obsessional neurosis, *Rat Man*. This gave his international recognition its start.

In December 1908, Stanley Hall, the founder of experimental psychology in the United States and president of Clark University in Worcester, Massachusetts, invited Freud to give a series of lectures for the 20th anniversary of the University's founding, which he would do in September 1909. Freud proposed that Ferenczi accompany him, but Hall also invited Jung. This was an immense success, and beginning in 1908, Freud took a lively interest in the development of psychoanalysis in America and regularly received news of it through Jones, Brill and Putnam.

Among his recent writings may be mentioned:

Psychopathology of Everyday Life (1901); *Jokes and Their Relation to the Unconscious*, written at the same time as his *Three Essays on the Theory of Sexuality* (1905). The latter caused a sensation. Judged particularly immoral, the book made Freud almost universally unpopular.

The years 1910–1914

Stimulated by this blossoming of psychoanalysis, Freud dreamt of creating a major association, greater than a local society, and he spoke of this, notably to Jung. The Second International Congress of Psychoanalysis was held in Nuremberg in March 1910. Ferenczi then proposed creating an international association with affiliates in different countries. In the closing days of this Congress, the existing psychoanalytical societies thereby joined the International Association, and other groups soon formed. In addition, with the collaboration of Rank and Sachs, the

14 Freud

project of creating a journal, *Imago*, devoted to the extra-medical applications of psychoanalysis became a reality in January 1912.

However, dissension and "divergences" also arose in the course of these same years. These had two characteristic traits: the dissidents rejected the essential psychoanalytical discoveries and formulated a different theory of the psychical structure. It was in 1912 that Freud found the break with Adler a relief and found himself forced to have Stekel resign toward the end of the year. In addition, his personal relations with Jung began to deteriorate. At the beginning of the year, Jung informed him of the intense uproar evident in Zurich's newspapers, where psychoanalysis was being violently attacked; this would be one of the reasons why a certain number of his Swiss disciples changed their attitude. Within this troubled context, Jones came up with the idea of creating a "Committee" and talked to Freud about this. It was a matter of forming a small group of trustworthy analysts, a sort of "old guard" around Freud, made up of Jones, Ferenczi, Abraham, Rank and Sachs. It began operating before the war, but it was after that it became very important for Freud, from both a scientific and administrative and a personal point of view. The first plenary meeting took place the following summer on May 25, 1913. During this same year, the Munich Congress saw the definitive break with Jung, then president of the International Association.

Totem and Taboo was published. In addition, the fact that it might be supposed that "schools of psychoanalysis" existed incited Freud to defend his work's name by publishing a polemical essay, *On the History of the Psycho-Analytic Movement*, in January and February 1914.

The war years (1914–1919)

According to Jones, when war was declared, Freud said he felt Austrian for the first time in thirty years. In March, he began writing a series of five papers on "metapsychology", a term he introduced in a letter to Fliess in 1896. He finished this in six weeks' time. Then he began to write a series of seven essays, which would be destroyed. He would write other articles, among them one on war and death. In 1916, he published the first part of *Introductory Lectures on Psycho-Analysis*, lectures he gave during the winter of 1916–1917. The second part of *Introductory Lectures on Psycho-Analysis* was completed, and the book appeared in June 1917.

Then came the defeat and fall of the Austro-Hungarian Empire, and Freud said that he could not keep himself from rejoicing about it.

In October 1919, Freud was named full professor at the University. He spoke of it as a "meaningless" title, because it did not give him the right to sit on the Faculty Council.

The years 1920–1930

The year 1920 began tragically with the death of Freud's daughter Sophie in January, at age 26, from an extremely bad case of pneumonia brought on by the flu.

Among his publications may be mentioned *Beyond the Pleasure Principle*, published in December, in which he introduced the notion of death instinct and that of repetition compulsion. In addition, he wrote *Group Psychology and the Analysis of the Ego*, which would appear in August 1921. In the course of that year, Freud accepted fewer patients because he received numerous students, principally from America and England, who wanted to learn his technique. Joan Riviere, in particular, translated *Introductory Lectures on Psycho-Analysis*, which was published that year and played a considerable role in the renewed interest in Freud's work after the war. In the English intellectual milieu, people were discussing his writings, which were then in vogue.

In April 1923, Freud had a cancerous tumour of his upper jaw and the right side of his palate removed. This was the first of thirty-three operations he would undergo during the rest of his life. His essay *The Ego and the Id* appeared during the same month. Then he published his *Autobiography*, written in August and September 1924. In 1926 he confronted some hard questions regarding the precise attitude to adopt toward analysts who were not physicians. In June, he had begun writing *The Question of Lay Analysis* when legal proceedings were brought against Theodor Reik, who was accused of charlatanism – charges which would come to nothing. One of the major writings published in 1927 was *The Future of an Illusion*; another was on fetishism. Finally, during the summer of 1929, he prepared *Civilization and Its Discontents*, which would be published at the beginning of 1930.

The years 1930–1939

The year 1930 was marked by the death of Freud's mother at the age of 95. In addition, he was awarded the Goethe Prize, for which he wrote a speech. In 1931, the disturbing rise of Nazism led to the exodus of more and more analysts to America, among them Alexander, who moved to Chicago; Rado went to New York, then Simmel to Los Angeles. In addition, Ferenczi worried Freud because he had changed his technique and was playing the role of a loving parent in an attempt to repair the unhappy early lives of his patients.

In March 1932, Freud decided to write a new series of *Lectures* in which he presented the evolution of his ideas over the course of the fifteen years following the publication of the first series. They actually appeared on December 6, 1932, but the publication was dated 1933.

During these years, Hitler's regime began to pose a threat to Austria, and it was proposed that Freud leave his country, something which he refused to do. The year 1934 saw the flight of the few Jewish analysts who were still in Germany and the "liquidation" of psychoanalysis there. Then, in 1935, theoretical and technical divergences arose among Viennese analysts close to Freud's ideas and the English, among them Jones. They involved, for example, the concept of death instinct, female sexuality, the phallic stage in the development of girls, but also the analysis of children, the conflict between Anna Freud and Melanie Klein. This is why Jones proposed regular meetings between the two

16 Freud

groups in order to compare their conceptions and discuss them, something which proved beneficial.

Political concerns and Freud's worsening health dominated the year 1937. All the same, he published: "Analysis terminable and interminable", "Constructions in analysis", and finally: *Moses, an Egyptian* (first issue of *Imago*); *If Moses Was an Egyptian* (fourth issue of *Imago*).

Then on March 11, 1938, the Nazis annexed Austria, which made Freud finally decide to accept Jones' invitation to leave Vienna and move with his family to London. So, with the collaboration of Jones, Marie Bonaparte, W. C. Bullit, then U.S. Ambassador to France, President Roosevelt, the Chargé d'affaires in Vienna, M. Wiley, the German ambassador to France, von Welczeck and also his fellow Italian psychoanalyst Eduardo Weiss, who had close ties with Mussolini, Freud succeeded in obtaining an exit visa. Notwithstanding, the Nazis were most intent upon extorting everything they could. Finally, possessing all the documents and exit visas, accompanied by his wife and his daughter Anna, Freud left Vienna definitively for Paris on the Orient Express, spent a day in Paris at Marie Bonaparte's, then arrived in London on June 6. He had succeeded in finishing the third part of his *Moses and Monotheism*, which then appeared in August 1938.

His final work, *An Outline of Psycho-Analysis* was never completed and was published in 1940.

He died on September 23, 1939, and his body was cremated at Golders Green Crematorium on the morning of September 26.

His creation: psychoanalysis

In his article "Psycho-Analysis" and "The Libido Theory" (1923), Freud defined *his* creation in this way:

> Psycho-Analysis is the name (1) of a procedure for the investigation of mental processes which are almost inaccessible in any other way, (2) of a method (based upon that investigation) for the treatment of neurotic disorders and (3) of a collection of psychological information obtained along those lines, which is gradually being accumulated into a new scientific discipline.[4]

Further on, he endeavoured to state both the "subject-matter" of his creation and the "foundations" of his theory:

> The assumption that there are unconscious mental processes, the recognition of the theory of resistance and repression, the appreciation of the importance of sexuality and of the OEdipus complex – these constitute the principal subject-matter of psycho-analysis and the foundations of its theory. No one who cannot accept them all should count himself a psycho-analyst.[5]

Before taking a look at the epistemological characteristics and foundations of this new human science with Paul-Laurent Assoun (1981), let us look at the political and sociocultural context within which it emerged, then, with Didier Anzieu (1959), at the role played by Freud's systematic self-analysis, starting with his father's death in October 1896 and correlative with its creation–discovery.

Political and sociocultural context

Austrian liberal bourgeois culture believed that humans were rational beings who would master nature through science and themselves through morality, two conditions necessary for creating a just society.

If, when it came to morality, it was sure of its right, virtuous and repressive, in politics, it was concerned about the rule of law and subjecting the social order and individual rights to it. While intellectually, it meant to subjugate the body to the mind, the path to social progress went by way of science, the education of the masses or *Bildung*, meaning the development of the life of the mind and the personality of individuals.

During the 1890s, and later at the turn of the 20th century, as Carl E. Schorske (1961) indicated in his remarkable book, *Fin-De-Siecle Vienna. Politics and Culture*, Viennese society was completely disintegrating under the impact of the crisis of liberalism and was threatened by mass political movements (Pan-Germanism and social Christianity), which considerably weakened the confidence that liberals had traditionally placed in their own legacy of rationality, moral law and progress. A culture of feeling, a *Gefühlskultur*, emerged then, coexisting alongside the moralistic culture of the European bourgeoisie and actually undermining it through its "amorality". In this way, it would shape the mentality of bourgeois artists and intellectuals and refine their sensibilities. Nonetheless, it also created problems. Within this combination of socio-political circumstances in Vienna, the *rational human being* had to yield to *the psychological human being*, a richer individual who allied reason with instinct and feeling and was therefore more dangerous and mercurial. The fate of the individual preoccupied its best writers (Arthur Schnitzler and Hugo von Hofmannsthal, for example), its artists (Gustav Klimt, Oskar Kokoschka and Arnold Schönberg, in particular) and its psychologists. A new view of human reality arose from it.[6]

For his part, Anzieu (1959) drew attention to the fact that since 1850 there had been a growing interest in dreams, hypnosis and dual personalities, and, since 1880, the same had been true of infantile sexuality and adult sexual perversions. In addition, at the end of the 19th century, a flood of sexual literature – scientific, fictional and sometimes pornographic – buffeted bourgeois morality. Finally, romanticism, philosophy, psychology and psychiatry increasingly used the notion of subconscious from a dynamic point of view.[7]

Within this tormented political and sociocultural context of *fin de siècle* in Vienna, Anzieu considered that Freud found himself alone in taking some decisive steps which would determine his creation, psychoanalysis.

18 Freud

Process of elaboration: from 1895 to 1902

The year of the publication of *Studies on Hysteria*, 1895, in itself, let me repeat, marked the beginnings of psychoanalysis. Recall also that the death of Freud's father in October 1896 was the event that led him to undertake his self-analysis, beginning in the summer of 1897, as well as to write *The Interpretation of Dreams*, published in 1900.

His systematic, intensive self-analysis, which was also a constant dialogue with his friend Fliess, precisely coincided, according to Anzieu, with "the very discovery of psychoanalysis itself".[8] It reached its peak in October 1897 and led both to the discovery of the OEdipus complex and to the recollection of his first childhood memories. While its dimension as self-therapy is obvious, it nevertheless remained secondary because, in relation to his psychotherapeutic practice, it was above all an exercise in supplying proof. It was in fact for Freud a matter of verifying in himself the existence and nature of the unconscious processes he detected in his patients. In return, the knowledge he acquired through them helped him in his self-analysis. A close interdependence existed between the two activities.[9]

Anzieu ultimately observed that Freud implicitly worked out the criteria for providing proof or guaranteeing objectivity in knowledge of the unconscious: the hypotheses explaining the unconscious psychical phenomena in fact require threefold verification: on patients (clinical data); on oneself (self-analytic data); and on cultural products testifying to collective unconscious determinations (mythological or literary data, for example).[10]

So, let us look at the discovery of the OEdipus complex.

It became apparent to Freud that in a certain obsessional male patient, his neurosis had developed around a desire for parricide, representing the elimination of the rival for the incestuous possession of the mother. But he also discovered and understood that he, like his patients, felt an incestuous desire for his mother and correlatively a desire for parricide, a desire that the work of mourning following the death of his father brought him to relive more and more intensely. From that time on, he became conscious that children experience these two desires as forbidden. Finally, the cultural reference represented by Sophocles' tragedy supplied him with its literary expression.

With the ending of his self-analysis in 1902, Freud underwent a series of psychical transformations and, according to Anzieu, really put into place the fundamental elements of psychoanalysis, both as a theory of the psychical apparatus and functioning and as a therapeutic technique. Notably, he developed a schema of the psychical apparatus involving three systems and two censorships – spaces of dynamic conflicts and circulation of energy, both free and bound. He was also readying himself to develop the theory of the libido. In addition, having recognized the specificity of psychical processes, he knew from then on that providing a psychoanalytical explanation of a phenomenon was to give an account of it from four points of view (dynamic, economic, genetic, topographical), without calling them this yet; this would have to wait until his *Metapsychology* of 1915.

His conceptual enrichment was then considerable. Indeed, still according to Anzieu's research, if about half of his conceptual capital in 1895 came from Helmholtz, Herbart, Charcot, Breuer and the psychiatry or psychology of the time, twice as many psychoanalytical notions were acquired between 1895 and 1902, and these principally resulted from his own creativity. Many of these new notions were still only brief, non-conceptualised or unpublished insights. Freud stored them and spent the next twenty years drawing on this reserve to develop his early theory of psychoanalysis.[11]

Finally, along with Anzieu, we find that Freud's hypotheses often came to him in the form of pairs of opposites, such as: psychical quantity/quality; representation of things/representation of words; latent content/manifest content; primary/secondary process; displacement/condensation, primary/secondary gain from illness; first/second censorship; hallucination/discharge (or even perception/motricity); auto-erotism/allo-erotism; activity/passivity; and male/female, just to cite the most important ones.

Epistemological characteristics and foundations of psychoanalysis

From the start, Freud situated psychoanalysis within the family of the natural sciences (*die Naturwissenschaften*), the sciences strictly speaking, adopting their explanatory rationality, in contrast to the family of the "sciences of the mind (*die Geisteswissenschaften*), tempted by totalising worldviews, to which it would nonetheless make a contribution. In his *Freud et les sciences sociales* (1993), Paul-Laurent Assoun considered that by drawing upon this contrast between the *Naturwissenschaften* and the *Geisteswissenschaften*, Freud takes up a pair of opposites that had been formed during a long epistemological debate, something which it is important to keep in view in order to grasp how psychoanalysis was heir to this debate and how it differed from it.[12] He in fact explains that this debate, known as the battle of the methods, and particularly developed in Germany, was full-fledged at just about the time of the birth of psychoanalysis. Moreover, he emphasised that it was Wilhelm Dilthey, founder of an epistemology of the human sciences, who proposed to differentiate between these two scientific domains in terms of their objects, their methods – explanatory for the natural sciences and comprehensive and interpretative for the sciences of the mind – and the type of rationality involved.

In his remarkable book *Introduction à l'épistémologie freudienne* (1981),[13] Assoun reminded us that Freud developed his analytical knowledge using conceptual and terminological material borrowed from 19th-century epistemological references and models, those of his mentors, to whom he remained attached all throughout his life.

20 Freud

The epistemological foundations of the Freudian creation would be of three kinds: monistic, physicalist and agnostic.

Its monistic foundation presupposes that psychoanalysis, a natural science, rejects the battle of the methods and therefore any sort of dualism. For it, *interpretation is an explanation*. There was therefore no reason to split the psychoanalytical approach into an explanatory part and an interpretative part.

Its physicalist foundation refers to the founding physico-chemical model. Indeed, the very name "psychoanalysis" came about through direct analogy with this model. Analysis signifies "decomposition", "taking apart", and the basis of the analogy with chemistry is atomistic representation: the instincts, as components of psychic life, are comparable to the ultimate constituents of matter, which are reducible to force. So, this natural science, unfolding in accordance with the psychology–physiology–physics sequence, rested on a strong determinist need to assign a cause and reconstruct the process.

Finally, *its agnostic foundation* pertains to Freud's endorsement of the scientific nature of psychoanalytical knowledge, all the while asserting that there is an absolute limit to knowledge of the unconscious. As Assoun has emphasised, we are at the heart of the paradox of Freud's epistemology, and he elaborated his metapsychology in this way to overcome the contradiction between the phenomenal requirement inherent in psychoanalysis as a natural science and the "trans-objectivity" it deals with, the study of unconscious processes as they show through phenomena.

What, then, is the structure of this Freudian epistemological identity embodied in *metapsychology* and its three dimensions (topographical, dynamic and economic), and what are its models?

Freud engaged in a whole thought process going from anatomo-physiology to the *topographical* defended and inspired by one of his mentors, the physiologist Ernst Brücke. He later transferred his positivist stance and his technique of observation onto the clinic. The physiological is first understandable on the basis of anatomical structure.

The dynamic dimension was inspired by the Herbartian model elaborated within a tradition of German psychology dating back to the beginning of the 19th century to Johann Friedrich Herbart, who considered that the psyche could be investigated because it had an atom, a basic motion called *representation*. *All psychical facts are representative*. Freud therefore borrowed a language and categories from Herbart, and when he made representation the basis of psychical activity, he updated this Herbartian schema with all its dynamic connotations. As for the quota of affect, it is an integral part of the psychic process, remaining essentially representational. Consequently, Herbart introduced the properly psychological dimension into the metapsychological object.

Finally, Assoun has observed that the *economic* is rooted in the "Fechnero–Helmholtzian" model. By attributing a quantitative dimension to psychic phenomena, as well as requiring quantification, Freud updated the issues of

19th-century scientific psychology. This is what made the theory of the libido, in particular, the basis of the metapsychological edifice. Let us remember that Gustav Fechner was the founder of psychophysics and Hermann von Helmholtz an eminent physiologist. The connection between physiology and psychology went by way of quantification. The fundamental principles of Freudian energetics derive directly from Fechnerian energetics. Freud thus specified the principle of stability as a principle of constancy–inertia. The energetic connotations of Freud's vocabulary – investment, discharge, abreaction, libido, quota of affect, for example – also deserve to be emphasised.

Freud's attraction to the monism of Ernst Haeckel, a German Darwinist, scientific and cultural reference, also deserves mention. In Germany, Haeckel was a famous and influential scientist of his time and his ideas expanded in the intellectual and cultural milieu. Therefore, he became a scientific and cultural referential and influential figure.

Finally, in several texts, Freud writes about "the bridge" between psychoanalysis and the sciences of the mind. In particular, *The Interpretation of Dreams* shows that the psychical processes at work in dream-work are just as active in pathological phenomena as in cultural products, through the universal symbolic, for example. Consequently, the application of psychoanalysis to the sciences of the mind would, in Freud's eyes, be proof that it cannot be reduced to a psychopathology and that it therefore has something to say, not only about symptoms, but also about normal psychic functioning and beyond that about cultural products. Psychoanalysis acquires a mediating function between the medical sciences and the sciences of the mind by linking the two. This is what Freud expressed once again in "Psycho-Analysis" (1926), writing that there had not

> been space to allude to the applications of psycho-analysis, which originated, as we have seen, in the sphere of medicine, to other departments of knowledge (such as Social Anthropology, the Study of Religion, Literary History and Education) where its influence is constantly increasing. It is enough to say that psycho-analysis, in its character of the psychology of the deepest, unconscious mental acts, promises to become the link between Psychiatry and all of these other branches of mental science.[14]

Thus, for Freud, the unfolding of the essence of psychoanalysis presupposed a path leading toward the medical sciences, but also toward the sciences of the mind, affirming, consequently, his twofold epistemological affiliation, as Assoun explained so nicely in his *Freud et les sciences sociales* (1993).

Of course, but when Freud wrote about the relationships that psychoanalytical work weaves with the other sciences of the mind (mythology, linguistics, folklore, psychology of peoples and sciences of religions, in particular), he did not seem to envisage either genuine reciprocity or, even less, relationships of

22 Freud

equality, because as he wrote in "Symbolism in Dreams", in *Introductory Lectures on Psycho-Analysis*:

> In all these links the share of psycho-analysis is in the first instance that of giver and only to a less extent that of receiver. It is true that this brings it an advantage in the fact that its strange findings become more familiar when they are met with again in other fields; but on the whole it is psycho-analysis which provides the technical methods and the points of view whose application in these other fields should prove fruitful. The mental life of human individuals, when subjected to psycho-analytic investigation, offers us the explanations with the help of which we are able to solve a number of riddles in the life of human communities or at least to set them in a true light.[15]

Once again, the scientific nature of the discourse is permeated with determining factors and issues of an ideological and identity nature correlative to the creation of any science. We shall encounter this type of discourse again in Durkheim, whose biographical journey and creation we are now going to discover.

Notes

1 Ernest Jones, *Sigmund Freud: Life and Work. Vol 1: The Young Freud 1856–1900. Vol 2: The Years of Maturity 1901–1919. Vol 3: The Last Phase 1919–1939*, London, Hogarth Press, 1953–1957.
2 Didier Anzieu, *Freud's Self-Analysis*, London, Hogarth Press and the Institute of Psycho-Analysis, 1986 (1959), p. 457.
3 *Ibid.*, p. 554.
4 Sigmund Freud, "Psycho-Analysis", S.E., 18, London: Hogarth, 1923, p. 235.
5 *Ibid.*, p. 247.
6 Carl E. Schorske, *Fin-De-Siecle Vienna. Politics and Culture*. New York, Vintage Books, 1981, pp. 4, 9–10.
7 *Op. cit.*, Anzieu, p. 571.
8 *Ibid.*, p. 568.
9 *Ibid.*, pp. 278, 247.
10 *Ibid.*, p. 568.
11 *Ibid.*, p. 566.
12 Paul-Laurent Assoun, *Freud et les sciences sociales*. Paris: Armand Colin, 1993, p. 13.
13 Paul-Laurent Assoun, *Introduction à l'épistémologie freudienne*, Paris, Payot, 1981.
14 Sigmund Freud (1926f). "Psycho-Analysis", S.E., 20. London: Hogarth, pp. 268–269.
15 Sigmund Freud, "Symbolism in Dreams, Lecture X," *Introductory Lectures on Psycho-Analysis* (Parts I and II). S.E., 15. London: Hogarth, 1915–1916, p. 168.

2

DURKHEIM

Biographical journey

Using Marcel Fournier's *Émile Durkheim: A Biography*.[1]
David Émile Durkheim was born on April 15, 1858 in Epinal (Vosges).

Family

Born in 1805 in Haguenau in Alsace, his father Moïse became a rabbi in Epinal in 1829, the first of a new community which took root on traditionally Catholic soil. Moïse's father, Israël David, was first a schoolteacher, then a rabbi in Mutzig, in Alsace.

Moïse Durkheim married Mélanie Isidor, born in 1820 in Charmes. He was 32 years old and his wife 17. It was a wedding of religion and business. Mélanie's father was a horse dealer in Charmes, where he settled down in 1802. Moïse and Mélanie belonged to a Germanic Alsatian family and moved to Epinal, into a world of Latin culture. They had five children: Desiré (who died at the age of 1), Rosine, Joseph-Félix, Cécile and Émile. For at least two generations, the Durkheim family would be associated with the field of embroidery and the textile business.

Childhood and adolescence

The upbringing Émile received stressed the sense of duty and responsibility and imparted to him the meaning of effort. He seemed to be a reserved, very sensitive child. He learned Hebrew, made his bar-mitzvah, participated regularly in Sabbath day and holy days celebrations, and familiarised himself with the Pentateuch and the Talmud. Furthermore, his father intended to have him to

24 Durkheim

carry on the family tradition of the rabbinate. Émile's first experience of Judaism was initially that of a religion which was not merely a system of ideas, but also a set of ritual practices. He developed a liking for collective life.

When the Franco–Prussian War broke out in 1870, Émile was 12 years old and found himself directly confronted with anti-Semitism.

During his schoolyears, probably between the age of 13 and 16, he underwent a crisis which led him to refuse to satisfy his father's wishes and to decide to study to be a teacher. Though taken aback, his father did not oppose his choice. Émile chose the École normale supérieure and therefore had to leave Epinal to take preparatory classes in Paris. He enrolled in preparatory courses at the Lycée Louis-le-Grand in the fall of 1876. Nevertheless, it would only be in the summer of 1879, after his third try, that he would finally be admitted to the École normale supérieure.

The École normale supérieure and the road toward sociology

In the fall of 1879, he entered the École normale supérieure, where he met Jean Jaurès and Henri Bergson, but also Pierre Janet, illustrious figures of the future. He then came to admire and be influenced by two history professors: Gabriel Monod and Fustel de Coulanges. The latter, a pioneer in social and economic history, considered history to be the science of social facts, that is to say, sociology itself. It was to analyse society as a whole, something he had endeavoured to show in *The Ancient City* (1864).[2]

Two others would have a notable influence on him: Émile Boutroux, a neo-Kantian philosophy professor, and Charles Renouvier, a "positivist", like Auguste Comte, whose influence on the French republic's intellectuals was considerable at the end of the 19th century. Boutroux was interested in the philosophy of science and defended the thesis of the coexistence of different levels or orders of reality, each one being relatively autonomous in relation to the others. Durkheim was receptive to this idea and would later apply it to his sociology, just as he would embrace Renouvier's proposition that a whole is not equal to the sum of its parts. Comte would quite obviously also be a major influence on him.

Durkheim had already decided to devote his efforts to studying the social question during his years at the École normale supérieure. But, beforehand, equipped with his *agrégation*, he was initially inclined toward secondary school teaching and obtained his first position as a philosophy professor at the Lycée of Le Puy in October 1882 and the following month at the Lycée of Sens. He began working on his doctoral thesis in 1883. While seeking to define the object (the relationships existing between the individual and society), he worked out a preliminary outline of what would become *The Division of Labor in Society*.[3]

He then filled his mind with the thought and methods of a certain number of noted thinkers of his time, among whom figured Alfred Fouillée, who used notions and dealt with ideas which would be at the heart of Durkheim's undertakings, something I shall return to later on. Claude Bernard, Wilhelm Wundt and Herbert Spencer, all of whom influenced him greatly, also deserve mention. He had in fact already manifested a concern for scientificity, the recourse to methods of experimentation and the objective study of the world through the discovery of laws. In addition, he expanded his field of interest to the "new" psychology, anthropology and the moral sciences. However, his work remained philosophical in nature.

It was in 1885 that he first came across the work of the anthropologists, notably that of Edward Tylor and Henry Morgan. In addition, his friend Lucien Herr helped him a great deal bibliographically by leading him to discover the writings of Robertson Smith and James Frazer published in the *British Encyclopaedia*.

Nevertheless, still searching for his path in life, he thought at this time of dividing his life between research into pure science and politics. Durkheim in fact keenly shared the social and political concerns of his fellow citizens: anarchy and divided opinions which in fact seemed to threaten the country's unity, but also manifestations of a virulent patriotism and signs heralding anti-Semitism through the publication in 1883 of the weekly *L'Antisémite*, not to mention the rise of individualism. Durkheim seemed very pessimistic with regard to the evolution of his society and also felt the need to act, something which politics would enable him to do.

Within this context, the choice of sociology could satisfy his dual need for knowledge and action. Like several of his colleagues, he was fascinated by the German university model, whose efforts to respect the infinite complexity of facts and extensively develop sociological investigation he admired. He then decided to leave for Germany after a meeting with Louis Liard, the director of higher education. At the time, it was a matter of an obligatory rite of passage. He was therefore granted leave for the 1885–1886 academic year and, before traveling to Germany in January 1886, went to live in Paris for the first semester, where he undertook to write the "first draft" of his doctoral thesis. He attended Théodule Ribot's lectures at the Sorbonne, read Charcot's writings and also discovered psychophysiology. When he left for Germany, Ribot recommended him to Wundt.

Teaching in Bordeaux

Upon his return, he was offered a teaching position at the University of Bordeaux in 1887 as Alfred Espinas' successor. He would teach education and "social science". When he arrived in Bordeaux, he was 29 years old and had just recently married Louise Dreyfus.

His first social science course in December 1887, sociology's "birth certificate", in Fournier's estimation,[4] was devoted to the "initial problem" of sociology: social solidarity. He wondered what the bonds were that unite people to one another. He then expounded on the ideas dear to him that constituted the fundamental bases of his positivist sociology: the idea of social laws and of interdependence of social facts; the conception of society as a whole and as an

26 Durkheim

organism; the notion of "collective consciousness"; the criticism of finalised, linear evolutionism, but an evolutionist perspective toward social differentiation and individualisation; the idea of social pressure; and a sense of the complexity of things.

Durkheim submitted the manuscript of his doctoral thesis on March 24, 1892 and that of his Latin thesis in November of the same year. The defence would only take place a year later.

His reading of Montesquieu's *The Spirit of the Laws* enabled him to open the debate about sociology as a new science. *The Division of Labor in Society* is, according to Fournier, "at once a eulogy of specialization and a celebration of work. ... [Modern] man is ... defined by the work he does and the way he specializes".[5]

Between May and August 1894, he published a series of four articles in the *Revue philosophique* under the title "Les règles de la méthode sociologique". These four texts would then be anthologised in a work entitled *Les règles de la méthode sociologique* published by Alcan in 1895.[6] It included a project: that of creating a school and bringing a team of dynamic, competent researchers together around a single approach. This book thus had "all the characteristics of a manifesto",[7] according to Fournier.

Durkheim began teaching a new course in 1894–1895. This was his course on religion. The concern up until then had been a few scholars and erudite persons, but at the turn of the century, religion became the subject of public debates and Durkheim became aware of the importance of religion in the life of societies. During the spring of 1895, he undertook to write a book on suicide and embarked upon a plan for new sociological journal, while the following year, he introduced another completely new course: the history of socialism.

These years, 1895 and 1896, were a period of transition and uncertainty. Indeed, Durkheim was in fact exposed to numerous, vigorous criticisms, even from colleagues close to him, such as Lucien Herr and Charles Andler. In addition, his father died in February 1896 at the age of 91. Then, at the beginning of the summer, Marcel Mauss' father, Gerson Mauss, died at the age of 62. Deeply affected, Durkheim went through a period of distress at the same time he was absorbed in writing *Suicide*.[8] At the end of June 1896, nine years after his arrival at the University of Bordeaux, he finally succeeded in having a chair of social science created, the first in a French university.

Suicide was published by Alcan in March 1897, and this event was all the more important for the very young discipline that sociology was at the time. Durkheim undertook a vast empirical study with the support of his nephew Marcel Mauss and, with no prior expertise, began handling social statistics. For him, it was a matter of applying the principles elaborated and presented in *The Rules of Sociological Method*.

His project consisted, on the one hand, of exploring the most individual act from a sociological perspective and, on the other hand, of diagnosing the state of health of contemporary societies and peoples said to be civilised by positioning himself as a clinician of social reality.

L'Année sociologique

The idea for a new sociology journal did not originate with Durkheim himself, but with Célestin Bouglé, who, upon returning from Germany, launched the idea of founding an international journal for promoting sociology. After a conversation with his friend Paul Lapie, Bouglé went to urge Durkheim to set up *L'Année sociologique*. They begged him, he would also say, to be the editor. Durkheim himself would acknowledge this. Durkheim and Bouglé met in Paris in April 1896. The following month, Durkheim approached his publisher, Félix Alcan.[9] The undertaking would only start up at the beginning of 1897. His future collaborators would be: Gaston Richard, Célestin Bouglé, Paul Lapie, Dominique Parodi, Marcel Mauss, Henri Hubert, Paul Fauconnet and Albert Milhaud.

L'Année sociologique, according to Fournier, is generally considered to have marked the birth of a new scientific discipline, sociology, and would enable a new group of researchers to acquire greater visibility. This intellectual world was the one Durkheim had been creating for some ten years. First of all, there was the openness to diverse disciplines: history, law, anthropology, political economy, criminology, demography. Then, the carrying out of a research programme focussing on a few main themes: family, religion, morality, crime and punishment. Finally, primacy was accorded to methodological issues.[10] For this team, it was a matter of defending their conception of sociology, its aim and its method. In addition, the creation of this journal would have to contribute to the institutionalisation of sociology, that is to say to the constitution of an autonomous discipline with its researchers, its places of production and exchanges and its research programmes. However, the two specialised areas of greatest interest to Durkheim and his collaborators were juridical and moral sociology and religious sociology.

The first volume was printed at the end of February 1898. In it Durkheim published his essay entitled "La prohibition de l'inceste et ses origines".

In the preface, according to Fournier, Durkheim clearly indicated the goal of the new journal as being to present a complete picture of sociology and its various currents, of course, but also, and above all, to inform sociologists regularly about research being performed in the special sciences, history of law, customs, religion, moral statistics, economics and so on. In other words, it was a matter of periodically inventorying all such research all the while "indicating what profit sociology can reap" from them.[11]

The years 1900–1910: professor at the Sorbonne

Durkheim's mother, Mélanie Durkheim, died on July 31, 1902, and that same year he applied for the chair of Education at the Sorbonne, to which he would be appointed. On December 4, he gave his inaugural lecture.

At this beginning of the 20th century, the position of Durkheim and of his collaborators in academia and in the intellectual field was assured as much by appointments to university positions, managing a journal and the access to several other

28 Durkheim

journals as by the group's large, diversified network of connections in political and intellectual milieu. Nevertheless, their adversaries were also more numerous and more virulent. In addition, his appointment enabled him better to find a place in the administration of higher education, to exercise greater influence in the academic world and to broaden his sphere of influence. Philosophers considered him to be one of their own and recognised the philosophical merit of his work.

At the Sorbonne, Durkheim intended to continue teaching about the questions of morality and moral education that remained at the heart of his preoccupations. So, beginning with the 1904–1905 academic year, he undertook to teach his major lecture course on the history of secondary education in France. Educational reform was in fact at the heart of the French Republic's project, and the situation was such that he did not hesitate to speak of a very serious crisis, which was particularly true for secondary education.[12]

He was then promoted to full professor beginning on November 1, 1906 and volume 10 of *L'Année*, the last volume to adhere to the original formula, was published in 1907.[13]

While Durkheim did not become involved in the political activities of the socialist group, he gave a great many public lectures between 1907 and 1909 dealing with diverse political issues: notably the religious question, pacifism and patriotism, judicial reform, the teaching of law, the status of civil servants, parliamentary impotence, science and religion.

It was in 1907 that he undertook the research that would lead to the publication of *The Elementary Forms of Religious Life* in 1912.[14] In 1908, the new formula of the *L'Année* debuted as a triennial publication and without the original essays, which would be published in book form by Alcan in the "Travaux de L'Année sociologique" series. Then, in 1909, he returned to the question of divorce and marriage, which he considered a disciplining of sexual life and a social institution because, more than a mere union between individuals, it was the basis of the family.[15]

His last years

Elementary Forms of Religious Life was finally published in 1912.

On August 1, 1914, Germany declared war on Russia and the next day on France. His son André was mobilised then and died on February 24, 1916.

Durkheim died on November 15, 1917.

His creation: the French school of sociology

The situation of sociology in France, according to Durkheim

Durkheim maintained that sociology was born in France. As he wrote, "it was born among us, and, although there is no country today where it is not being cultivated, it nevertheless remains an essentially French science".[16] Moreover, it could not emerge until the idea of determinism, which had been securely established in the physical and natural sciences, was finally extended to the social order. This extension occurred in the eighteenth century under the influence of the philosophy of the Encyclopédie.[17]

In "Lo stato attuale degli studi sociologici in Francia" ("The Present State of Sociological Studies in France") of 1895,[18] he presented the principal sociological theories and the three groups within which specialists in contemporary sociology had been evolving since the resumption of this work beginning in the 1870s: the "ethnographical and anthropological group", the "criminologist group" and the "academic group".

The "ethnographical and anthropological group" included all the work in sociology connected with the Société d'anthropologie de Paris, founded in 1859 by Paul Broca (1824–1880), a physician–surgeon and professor at the Faculté de médecine in Paris. While the Museum and Anthropology laboratory at the École pratique des hautes études were created in 1868, 1875 saw the opening of the doors of École d'anthropologie de Paris.

Having begun with anatomical studies, this anthropology extended its field of research a great deal to become a new total science of human beings, including prehistory, linguistics, ethnography, demography, geography and sociology integrating ethnographical sociology. A chair was then created in 1885, held by Charles Letourneau, who may be considered the principal representative of that group. He began to study the principal social institutions one after the other so as to reconstitute their historical development. Nevertheless, faithful to the spirit of the anthropological school, he strove to establish the relationships that they have with the different human races while following the evolution in time.

According to Durkheim, their viewpoint was largely deterministic, racial and inegalitarian in the sense that it supposed that each physical race corresponds to a degree of human evolution, of mental development and, therefore, of social organisation.

The "criminologist group" was composed of experts which criminology had led to sociology. Its organ was the *Archives d'anthropologie criminelle*; the two editors of this journal, Alexandre Lacassagne and Gabriel Tarde, were its primary sources of inspiration.

Gabriel Tarde (1843–1905) has traditionally been presented as the principal advocate of individualistic resistance to Durkheimian "sociologism". The first writings of this former magistrate pertained to the field of criminology. In 1894, he became the director of criminal statistics at the Ministry of Justice. His sociology was entirely constructed on the basis of the phenomenon of imitation, which makes possible the spreading of desires and beliefs from individual to individual, and precisely through that leads to the uniformisation of the group and its cohesion. The emphasis was therefore placed doubly on the individual by constituting him or her, on the one hand, as an imitative pole and, on the other hand, by setting him or her at the origin of every inventive social current destined, or not

30 Durkheim

destined, to be imitated. According to Durkheim's interpretation, Tarde's basic individualism did not in fact enable him to isolate the specific nature of social reality, insofar as an individual psychological phenomenon, even if it implies a dynamic of spreading, is, as a matter of principle, incapable of accounting for the specific nature of the social. Moreover, in Durkheim's opinion, Tarde had gone back Spencer's and Espinas' "philosophical" sophistry by affirming the validity of a single law in the formation of social groups and deriving all social laws from this original matrix.

Finally, he talked about the "academic group", essentially composed of philosophy professors.

Alfred Espinas (1844–1922), the first to be attracted to sociology, reconnected with the tradition interrupted in France after Comte and brought fresh life to the general problems of sociology by drawing inspiration from Spencer's work and progress made by the evolutionist hypothesis. In his book *Les sociétés animales* (1878), he considered that the social realm emerges as a sort of flowering of the biological realm to which it was attached without solution of continuity. Likening human society to an organism in this way, he gave sociology the idea of collective consciousness, which would be taken up by Alfred Fouillée.

For his part, Fouillée (1838–1912) made himself the advocate of social science in a book published in 1880, *La Science sociale contemporaine*. He developed a conception of society as an organism whose component parts are in relationships of mutual dependence, united then among themselves by voluntary and contractual bonds, hence the notions of consensus and social bond. He also introduced those of representation, social or collective consciousness and mechanical solidarity, which he contrasts with voluntary solidarity. But he considered that society is also defined by association, a key notion of psychology of intelligence, notably in English psychology, among the representatives of associationism, such as Alexander Bain.

Espinas and Fouillée above all devoted themselves to the most general problems connected with the nature of societies, social evolution and the relations of the social realm with the biological realm.

Durkheim also cited Frédéric Le Play (1806–1882), who in 1855 created the first *Société d'economie sociale* to promote the systematic observation of families and a whole series of reforms. His organs were *La réforme sociale* and *La science sociale*. His writings on *European workers* deserve mention. Nevertheless, he considered that Le Play was completely outside the intellectual movement that gave birth to this science and that his concerns were to a large extent apologetic in nature.

A brief evolving overview

During the 1890s, sociology flourished in an encouraging way which, other than France, reached various European countries (Italy, Spain, Belgium), but also the United States; the University of Chicago published the *American Journal of Sociology*. Indeed, those years were marked, notably, by the creation of journals, the founding of centres and institutes, the publication of new books. Thus, in France, the year 1895 saw the publication of books by Tarde, *La Logique sociale*, and Gustave Le Bon, *Psychologie des foules*. However, sociology was still far from enjoying the institutional and intellectual status of disciplines such as political economy or even anthropology.

At the beginning of the 20th century, sociology was fashionable, and Durkheim defended the idea that it was a matter of an "essentially French" science and not, as some would have people believe, a German one. Of course, it was still not well institutionalised as a discipline. There was neither any chair of sociology nor any place for training in sociological research, and its dynamism was the matter of the action of more or less isolated individuals and more or less marginal institutions. Moreover, the sociological scene had scarcely changed since Durkheim's arrival on it, since its principal competitors, ever very active, remained the same: Le Bon, Worms and Tarde.

Conditions, sources of inspiration and characteristics of the Durkheimian revolution

According to Fournier (2007), Durkheim came at a turning point in scientific thought because biology, which had just adopted the experimental method, was becoming a standard point of reference for philosophers.[19] Particularly noteworthy in this respect was the publication of Claude Bernard's *Introduction à l'étude de la médecine expérimentale* in 1865. In addition, the works of Charles Darwin (*The Origin of Species*, 1859) and Spencer were becoming known in France. The latter's evolutionary philosophy received a great deal of attention. It was the major philosophical event from 1870 to 1890, and his main works were translated into French. In particular, his *The Study of Sociology* (1873)[20] would contribute to giving sociology a place among the empirical sciences.

In *The Rules of Sociological Method*, Durkheim reminded us that "sociology sprang from the great philosophical doctrines";[21] and Fournier considers that it was the discovery and critique of political economy that conditioned Durkheim's passage from philosophy to sociology. For his part, the sociologist Tarot (1999) considers that Durkheim presented his sociological project as a *rupture* and a *creation*. Indeed, he thinks that Durkheim needed to found a School and in fact placed emphasis on the break for strategic reasons. He needed to *institute* sociology, *both in face of* and *against* philosophy, psychology and, above all, social psychology, but also the anthropogeography of the German school. According to Tarot, there were two issues at stake there: on the one hand, the political issue, since it was a matter of acquiring recognition through academic legitimacy; and, on the other hand, an epistemological issue, because it was important for him to show that this sociology had its own object, which is its alone since it alone would deal with it scientifically.

Thus, Durkheimism was first of all a theoretical project consisting of introducing scientific rationalism and the experimental method into the study of

32 Durkheim

social facts, the idea of which, as Tarot (1999) has reminded us, dated back to the Ideologists, even to Condorcet. Since the law of causality had been proven for the other realms of nature and in recent times in the psychological world, Durkheim believed that there was reason to concede that it was also true of the social world. Indeed, understanding society as a *natural reality* was first of all situating social phenomena within the continuum of natural phenomena. It was showing that the human world belonged to the world of living beings. Durkheim formulated this expressly in "Sociology" (1915), pursuing the thought of the encyclopaedists, and above all that of Saint-Simon, whom he considered had been the first to have formulated it, the first to declare that human societies are assuredly unique realities and different from those found in the rest of nature, but subject to the same determinism. Social organisms must therefore be the object of a science comparable to that dealing with individual organisms and, for this reason, he proposed naming it *social physiology*.[22] Durkheim went on to explain the decisive role Auguste Comte played in the creation of this new science. A new science, Durkheim said, came to be added to the complete system of the sciences. Saint-Simon had heralded it, but it was Comte who fathered it. It was through him that it began to exist. He is also the one who named it sociology, which some may find a poor choice. It is, however, irreplaceable, because it designates not just any study of social beings but only such studies conducted in a spirit analogous to that reigning in the other natural sciences.[23]

However, while always referring to the models and experiments of the other existing sciences, biology and psychology in particular, it was also necessary for sociology to *single itself out* and *become autonomous*, therefore creating its own identity and its *raison d'être* by having as subject matter and epistemological field an order of facts left unstudied by the other sciences. This is why sociology must be a discipline which is neither a chapter of psychology – although, paradoxically, resorting to this discipline was to his mind indispensable – nor subordinate to biology. It was to be an independent "science" having its *own object*, society. Moreover, in "Sociology and Its Scientific Field" (1900),[24] Durkheim laid down a proposition to be taken as an axiom which establishes the identity and epistemological foundations of sociology as an autonomous, distinct science, in relation to psychology in particular; however, according to his *Suicide*, a social psychology has its own laws,[25] something which does not, *in fine*, make his position particularly clear. According to this proposition,

> For sociology, properly speaking, to exist, there must occur in every society phenomena of which this society is the specific cause, phenomena which would not exist if this society did not exist and which are what they are only because the society is constituted the way it is.[26]

The corollary of this proposition, Durkheim continues, is that social phenomena do not have their determining, immediate cause in the nature of individuals.[27]

Otherwise, sociology would in fact become confused with psychology. This sociological point of view thus implies that the two terms "individual" and "society" are postulated from the beginning as inseparable.[28]

He clarified this thought, which did not seem quite clear in the eyes of his detractors, by saying, "I have repeated a number of times that to place sociology outside of individual psychology was simply to say that it constituted a *special psychology*, having its own subject matter and a distinctive method".[29]

In addition, Durkheim considered that among the most important advances that sociology had to make remained the acquisition by all sociologists of the sense of the specificity of social reality, that is, of an understanding of social facts that only sociological knowledge can confer. Notably, it is consequently impossible "for the same notions to fit identically things of a different nature".[30] This is why entirely new concepts must be created that are suited to the needs of science and expressed with the help of a special terminology.

Additionally, the criticism he made of the sociology of his time was twofold:

- on the one hand, there was the lack of method and precise results, the paucity of information and the generality of the conclusions. He explained, notably, that sociologists have generally only seen social facts as derived psychical facts, that is to say, expanded and generalised, while he would establish that there is a dividing line between the former and latter analogous to that separating the biological realm from the mineral realm;[31]
- on the other hand, there was an illusion of wanting to deduce practical reforms from the theory and the artificial, ambitious nature of these reforms.

This is why he wanted to introduce into sociology a "reform" similar to the one that had transformed psychology over the past thirty years. Indeed, introspective up until then, the birth of objective psychology or "psychological naturalism" spawned the great revolution consisting of the fundamental rule of finally studying mental facts or states of consciousness, exclusively from the outside and no longer from the point of view of the consciousness experiencing them.

The German social and moral sciences, including the work of the "academic socialism" of Adolf Wagner and Gustav von Schmoller, as well as that of Albert Schaeffle, to whom he felt close, represented another source of inspiration of his sociology; he considered this urgent to import, and it could obviously contribute to the development of sociology, something for which he would incur reproach.[32]

In this respect, he considered that the profoundly rationalistic French mind had a natural affinity with everything that is simple and for this reason ended up not wanting to accept complexity, even where it exists. As a result, in studying societies the French had focussed all their attention on the simple elements which had formed them, meaning the individual, and had tried to reduce the rest to this. They had thus been led to see collective being only as a plurality, a simple repetition of the individual. In contrast,

34 Durkheim

the Germans had always believed very profoundly that there was a sort of heterogeneity between individuals and society. While the German mind is admittedly more sensitive than the French mind to what is complex in social things, its analytical ability is also poor, which has made it impossible for the former to subject this complicated reality fully to scientific analysis This is why it has willingly concluded that this complexity of social facts is at least partially unintelligible.[33]

This is why he considered that, in face of social phenomena to be explored, a scientific sociology presupposes both the awareness that they are fairly complex – so that sociologists do not allow themselves be seduced by explanations which are too facile and too clear – and a rationalist state of mind.[34]

Ultimately, Durkheim's main goal was to enable sociology to gather the means necessary for it to be able to rank among the positive, genuinely objective sciences. Actually, he fairly quickly recognised that, owing to the overly general nature of his theories and to the lack of documentation, realising his goal sociology particularly needed history and its critical method, on the one hand, and ethnography, on the other, and was guided and supported in this by Mauss; both fields are suppliers of a quantity of facts accumulated, not to mention statistics. However, their scientificity being in no way assured, in his opinion, he proposed they transform themselves into social sciences by adopting his sociological method. By doing so and becoming more sociological, all these sciences would become truly social. Thus, as Tarot emphasized in *De Durkheim à Mauss, l'invention du symbolique*, Durkeim proposed to history comparatism that was at the heart of all the great intellectual adventures of the 19th century. To succeed, comparatism had to become more sociological by adopting Durkheimian sociological methods.

As for ethnology, Durkheim discovered the British evolutionist school of anthropology through James Frazer's article "Totemism" (1887). His criticism showed that it was not a social science. He saw perfectly that there was a critical problem of establishing the facts themselves, in particular. This is why he also envisaged introducing the sociological method into ethnology and, first of all, into ethnography, and then this "sociologised" ethnography into all of sociology. By imposing his sociological method, he consequently hastened anthropology's entry into another era of its history and of science, notably into the functionalism of Bronislaw Malinowski and Alfred Reginald Radcliffe-Brown later adopted by British social anthropology.

Society and social facts, the specific objects of Durkheimian sociology

Society

In *The Rules of Sociological Method* (1895), Durkheim reminded readers that society is not the mere sum of individuals, but the system formed by their association represents a specific reality which has its own characteristics. Undoubtedly no collective entity can be produced if there are no individual consciousnesses: this is a necessary but not a sufficient condition. In addition, these consciousnesses must be associated and combined, but combined in a certain way. It is from this combination that social life arises and consequently it is this combination which explains it. By aggregating together, interpenetrating, by fusing together, individuals give birth to a being, psychical if you will, but one which constitutes a psychical individuality of a new kind. Thus it is in the nature of that individuality and not in that of its component elements that we must search for the proximate and determining causes of the facts produced in it. The group thinks, feels and acts entirely differently from the ways its members would if they were isolated.[35]

Thus, every society constitutes a *sui generis* synthesis involving two sorts of distinct elements: the *contained*, characterised by the different phenomena occurring among the individuals associated, and the *container*, defined by the very association within which these phenomena are observed.[36]

According to Durkheim, the individuals therefore constitute the "substrate" of every society, and their association will produce "new phenomena" which consist of the very emergence of social facts of a specific, singular nature, distinct from the individual fact. They will have an impact on the individual consciousnesses by forming them to a large extent, something which brought him to say that "although society is nothing without individuals, each one of them is more a product of society than he is the author".[37]

From all that emerges, according to Tarot (1999), a *holistic* conception of the social in many senses of the term: in the sense in which society is prior to the individual; in the sense in which each society is a whole, something which implies that a certain cohesion of the whole is essential to its components; and finally, in the sense in which, a society being a whole, this whole develops new properties which are not the sum of the qualities of the individuals making it up. This third sense is clearly expressed in the organicist metaphors consistent with his functionalism.

Social facts

What is a social fact? This opening question was asked over and over in each of the writings of the founder of the French school of sociology – not only in his general or methodological writings but also in his particular and specific research.

For Durkheim, it was a matter of considering social phenomena as both a point of departure and as an immediate object of this science instead of starting from one or another mental state in order to arrive at them. Indeed, it is not to be forgotten that generally, and up until then, sociologists like Tarde, in particular,

36 Durkheim

but also the English anthropological school, as well as Wundt's *Völkerpsychologie*, only saw in these social phenomena derived, that is, generalised, expanded psychical facts.[38] However, Durkheim established that there is a dividing line between the former and the latter analogous to the one separating the biological from the mineral realm, and he set down a rule that a social phenomenon *can only be produced by another social phenomenon.* I shall come back to this at a later point.

So, social facts are to be found in the society itself that produces them, not in its members, and constitute *the matter* of social life. They differ not only *in quality* from individual, psychical facts, but have a different "substrate" – the group, simple or composite – they do not evolve in the same milieu and are not dependent on the same conditions.

They consist of ways of acting, thinking and feeling which *penetrate every individual by imposing themselves on him or her from the outside and by exercising external constraint on him or her.* The individual then finds them all constituted and must conform to this, given that every obligation presupposes a collective authority which obliges and exercises an ascendancy and a subject who acquiesces. Durkheim considered any fact presenting this characteristic as being *social* in nature. These "ways" then partake of the morale and material supremacy that society has over its members. "But in order for a social fact to exist", he explained, "several individuals at the very least must have interacted together and the resulting combination must have given rise to some new production".[39] He called that "very special kind of existence" "institution".[40]

In addition, he emphasised that in penetrating the individuals who are going to assimilate them, these phenomena, these institutions, beliefs or social practices, will necessarily undergo a *process of individualisation* through the marking of each one's unique nature, something which explains the fact that, up to a certain point, each of us forms his or her own religious faith, worship, morality or style. It is a matter therefore of "individual incarnations",[41] or of their private manifestations which one may confuse with the productions and collective states. They depend to a large extent upon "the psychical and organic constitution of the individual, and on the particular circumstances in which he is placed".[42] They are therefore not truly sociological phenomena. They pertain to two realms at the same time. Durkheim called them "*socio-psychical*".[43] They are of interest to sociologists all the same without being the immediate subject matter of sociology.

Works, collective as well as ancient, and invested with a particular authority that our upbringing has taught us to recognize and to respect, are generally transmitted to us ready-made by earlier generations. Nevertheless, consisting thus of ways of thinking, feeling and acting, it is incontestable that social facts are produced by a *sui generis* elaboration of psychical facts. This is, as Durkheim recognised, somewhat analogous to that which occurs in each individual consciousness and which progressively transforms the sensations, reflexes and instincts of which it is originally constituted. It is then that he takes these social facts back to "states of collective consciousness", which he calls "representations", said to be collective, in this instance, of another nature, and much more complex, than the states of the individual consciousness or individual representations. Hence his conception of social life essentially made up of these collective representations[44] – which come under the "mentality of groups" or "collective thought" – different from the individual mentality and having to be explored in itself and for its own sake in search of its own laws. With respect to this, Durkheim explained, the mode of expression of collective thought is the formula. What distinguishes it from the expression of individual thought is: 1. its impersonality: it is, as it were, stereotyped; 2. its imperativeness; 3. its rhythm: a formula is cadenced like a verse. It is because it is social in origin that it has these three characteristics.[45]

Finally, these collective representations, which above all translate collective realities – states of the collectivity – are products of the immense cooperation of a multitude of diverse minds which have associated and combined their ideas and their feelings across generations. They therefore depend on the way in which the collectivity is constituted and organised, on its morphology and on its economic, moral and religious institutions.

The Durkheimian discourse on the method

Durkheim drew attention to the fact that up until his time, sociologists had not been very concerned with defining and characterising the methods they applied to the study of social facts, hence the realisation that there was no method and there was an urgent need *to draw up some rules inspired by scientific rationalism which adapted the experimental method to the specific nature of social facts.* Durkheim laid them down with the intention of guaranteeing sociology's status as a *natural science.*

The principles of the Durkheimian method as set forth in *The Rules of Sociological Method* (1895) consist of a few rules relating to observation and its corollaries, to the distinction between the normal and the pathological and to explaining social facts and providing proof. Later, in 1908, in "Remarque sur la méthode en sociologie", he used two words to characterise it: "historical and objective".[46] It would therefore be historical, objective and comparative.

To begin with, he reminds us that sociology must give up the idea of immediately embracing the entirety of social reality, as well as its historical evolution, as a whole. He distinguished among three areas of sociology: *social morphology,* the goal of which is the study of material forms of society or social ways of being and, therefore, phenomena pertaining to morphological combinations; *social physiology,* which studies social ways of acting, or physiological or functional phenomena, which are much more varied and complex than the preceding ones; and, finally, *the study of collective representations.*[47]

Then, he considered that sociology would have to introduce analysis and progressively distinguish different parts, elements or aspects able to serve as the subject matter of special problems. He said that it had been their ambition to open up for sociology what Comte called the era of specialisation. A genuine division of labour was set up. The study of three groups of facts was particularly

38 Durkheim

undertaken: religious facts, moral and juridical facts and economic facts. Instead of doing sociology in general, some devoted themselves to religious sociology, others to juridical and moral sociology and others still to economic sociology.[48]

The first, most fundamental rule consisted of dealing with social facts in themselves from the outside, as things and not as concepts, by laying hold of them through their most objective characteristics in a state of mind similar to that of specialists in the natural sciences exploring their own field.

It is definitely because social phenomena form a natural realm as a prolongation of the living world that they had to be studied from the outside as other facts of nature. A *thing* is everything that is open and evident to observation. What is given to us, for example, is not this or that idea of the moral ideal, but it is the set of rules which actually determine conduct. Thus, sociologists must be in a state of ignorance and systematically reject all common sense prejudices, all parasitical preconceptions.

Moreover, since social facts are *social things*, the method is therefore exclusively sociological. Consequently, sociologists must endeavour to consider them from an angle in which they are in isolation from individual manifestations. Durkheim then appeals to history as a tool of sociological analysis prior to and conditioning the explanatory stage.

What is this *social thing* which is an institution in fact made of? It is history which plays this role, analogous to a microscope in the realm of physical realities.[49] This complex whole is constituted bit by bit; history thus makes apparent its diverse elements, born one after the other.

Moreover, Durkheim's use of the word "primitive" corresponds to a precise conceptualisation applied within the framework of what he called the genetic method. The *elementary*, with which the notion of the primitive is associated, is the simple, that is to say, the fundamental term apt to be made up of itself and to integrate into a more complex entity.

However, among these social facts, a distinction must be made between normal facts and pathological ones that are of the same nature but that all the same constitute two different varieties. This is why, he explained, "*a social fact is normal for a given social type, viewed at a given phase of its development, when it occurs in the average society of that species, considered at the corresponding phase of its evolution*".[50]

It would be the task of social morphology to constitute these species and to classify them into social types, leading to the truly explanatory part.

He particularly applied the above rules to crime, the pathological nature of which is recognised by all criminologists. Nevertheless, he observed that criminality exists, and has always existed, in all societies, as it is inherent to the fundamental conditions of all social life, no matter what forms it has taken. But it can also take abnormal forms due to its high rate in a given society.

Explaining a social phenomenon, according to Durkheim, requires a separate search for the efficient cause producing it, then for the function it fulfils, and requires dealing with the former before the latter. The bond of solidarity uniting cause and function has a reciprocal nature which has not been sufficiently recognized, hence following rule: "*The determining cause of a social fact must be sought among antecedent social facts, and not among the states of individual consciousness*".[51]

This is a two-sided anti-reductionist rule, Tarot has observed (1999), against both racialist or biologising reduction and against psychological reductions. Applying it brings out the irreducible complexity of social facts.

Its function can but be social, that is to say, productive of socially useful effects. Finally, the causes are to be looked for in the very constitution of this *internal social milieu*, made up of things (material objects, established customs and constituted law, among others) and of persons – the human milieu – which is a factor determining collective evolution, both through the volume of the society and through its dynamic density.

The aims of Durkheimian sociology

Durkheim's goal was to secure the specialisation of sociology to make it a genuine positive science. It would move in that direction. He reminded people, moreover, of the importance of a synthetic discipline whose role is to draw out from the diverse specialised disciplines certain general conclusions and certain synthetic conceptions apt to stimulate and inspire specialists and to lead to new discoveries which would in turn would contribute to the progress of philosophical thought. The goal he set for sociology, the mission he assigned to it, was to provide a set of guiding principles at the heart of our practice which give meaning to our action.

Systematic, pyramidal and *imperialistic*: this is how Tarot (1999) has described the Durkheimian conception of sociology's relationships with the other social sciences. It is part of a "self-centred scheme", because sociology decides from its own perspective and allots rules and places to other disciplines. He considers that this model owes its organic, systematic nature to the prestige of the natural sciences, and among them to the biological sciences of the time.

In the end, according to Tarot, Durkheim all the same revolutionised ethnology and influenced linguistics, which to a great extent owes to him its definition of language, as both a system and a social fact. He also shook up history, not only by assigning it new objects, out of which would come a good part of quantitative history, long-term history and the history of mentalities, but also by obliging it to rethink its methods and way of constructing facts.

Notes

1 Marcel Fournier, *Émile Durkheim: A Biography*, Cambridge UK, Polity Press, 2013.
2 Numa Denis Fustel de Coulanges, *The Ancient City*, Baltimore MD, Johns Hopkins Press, 1980 (1864).
3 Émile Durkheim, *Division of Labor in Society*, New York NY, The Free Press, 1997 (1893).

40 Durkheim

4 *Op. cit.*, Fournier, *Émile Durkheim: A Biography*, p. 106.
5 *Ibid.*, p. 151.
6 Published in English as *The Rules of Sociological Method*, New York NY, The Free Press, 1982 (1895).
7 *Op. cit.*, Fournier, *Émile Durkheim: A Biography*, p. 179.
8 Available in English as Durkheim, *Suicide, a Study in Sociology*, New York NY, The Free Press, 1951 (1897).
9 *Op. cit.*, Fournier, *Émile Durkheim: A Biography*, p. 261.
10 *Ibid.*, p. 275.
11 *Ibid.*, p. 274.
12 *Ibid.*, p. 472–73.
13 *Ibid.*, p. 527.
14 Émile Durkheim, *The Elementary Forms of Religious Life*, Oxford, Oxford University Press, 2001 (1912).
15 *Op. cit.*, Fournier, *Émile Durkheim: A Biography*, p. 544.
16 Émile Durkheim, "Sociology", *Émile Durkheim, 1858–1917: A Collection of Essays, with Translations and a Bibliography*, Kurt Wolff (ed.), Columbus OH, Ohio State University Press, 1960 (1900), p. 376.
17 *Ibid.*
18 Émile Durkheim, "Lo stato attuale degli studi sociologici in Francia", *La riforma sociale* 3, 1895, pp. 607–622, 691–707.
19 *Op. cit.*, Fournier, *Émile Durkheim: A Biography*, p. 179.
20 Herbert Spencer, *The Study of Sociology*, New York, D. Appleton & Co., 1873.
21 *Op. cit.*, Durkheim, *The Rules of Sociological Method*, p. 111.
22 *Op. cit.*, Durkheim, "Sociology". Durkheim makes many of these same points in "Sociology in France in the Nineteenth Century", in *Émile Durkheim on Morality and Society, Selected Writings*, Robert Bellah (ed.), Chicago, The University of Chicago Press, 1973 (1900), pp. 6–10.Sociology (1915): Extrait de La science française, Larousse et Ministère de l'Instruction publique et des beaux-arts, vol 1.
23 *Ibid.*
24 Émile Durkheim, "Sociology and Its Scientific Field," in *op. cit.*, Wolff (ed.), pp. 354–75 and as "The Realm of Sociology as a Science", *Social Forces* 59, 4, 1981, pp. 1054–70.
25 *Op. cit.*, Durkheim, *Suicide, a Study in Sociology*, p. 276.
26 *Op. cit.*, Durkheim "Sociology and Its Scientific Field", in *op. cit.*, Wolff (ed.), p. 363.
27 *Ibid.*
28 Émile Durkheim, "M. Aslan, *La Morale de Guyau*", *Revue de métaphysique et de morale* 14, supplément juillet: 14. Examination of thesis, 1906.
29 Émile Durkheim, "The Psychological Conception of Society (1901)", anthologised in *op. cit.*, Durkheim, *The Rules of Sociological Method*, p. 195.
30 *Op. cit.*, Durkheim, *The Rules of Sociological Method*, p. 114.
31 *Op. cit.*, Durkheim, "Lo stato attuale degli studi sociologici in Francia".
32 Émile Durkheim, "La Science positive de la morale en Allemagne", *Revue philosophique* 24, 1887, pp. 33–58, 113–142, 275–284, translated in Émile Durkheim (ed.) *Ethics and the Sociology of Morals: Émile Durkheim*, Buffalo NY, Prometheus Book, 1993.
33 *Op. cit.*, Durkheim, "Lo stato attuale degli studi sociologici in Francia".
34 *Ibid.*
35 *Op. cit.*, Durkheim, *The Rules of Sociological Method*, p. 86.
36 *Op. cit.*, Durkheim "Sociology and Its Scientific Field".
37 *Op. cit.*, Durkheim, *Division of Labor in Society*, p. 274.
38 *Op. cit.*, Durkheim, "Lo stato attuale degli studi sociologici in Francia".
39 *Op. cit.*, Durkheim, *The Rules of Sociological Method*, p. 15.
40 *Ibid.*

41 *Ibid.*, p. 23.
42 *Ibid.*, p. 24.
43 *Ibid.*, pp. 24, 99 n. 20.
44 *Op. cit.*, Durkheim, "The Psychological Conception of Society".
45 Émile Durkheim, "Leçons sur la morale". Notes taken by G. Davy of lectures on "La Morale" that Durkheim gave at the Sorbonne, probably from his 1908–1909 lecture course, translated in Steven Lukes' *Émile Durkheim: An Intellectual Biography* (thesis presented for the degree of Doctor of Philosophy, deposited at Bodleian Library in Oxford), vol. 2, 1968, pp. 248–260.
46 *Op. cit.*, Émile Durkheim, "Remarque sur la méthode en sociologie", *Textes*, vol. 1, Paris, Minuit, 1975 (1906), pp. 58–61, 58.
47 *Op. cit.*, Durkheim, "Sociology and Its Scientific Field".
48 *Op. cit.*, Durkheim, "Sociology".
49 *Op. cit.*, Durkheim, *Textes*, vol. 1, p. 59.
50 *Op. cit.*, Durkheim, *The Rules of Sociological Method*, p. 60.
51 *Ibid.*, p. 90.

3

MAUSS

Bibliographical journey

Using the biography written by Marcel Fournier *Marcel Mauss, A Biography.*[1] Marcel Israël Mauss was born in Epinal, France on May 10, 1872.

Family

His father, Gerson, born in the Bas-Rhin, France, married Rosine Durkheim, Émile's older sister. He was 37 years old at the time and his wife was 23.

Marcel, the nephew of Émile Durkheim, had a younger brother, Camille Henri, who was born on June 10, 1876.

The Mauss family worked in the textile sector and the father was the business representative for a drapery company.[2]

Childhood and adolescence

Like other young Jews of his generation, he received a religious education, learned Hebrew and made his bar-mitzvah. He stopped practising his religion at about the age of 18. He played sports, swam, ran, boxed and fenced.[3]

After receiving an excellent classical secondary education at the Lycée of Epinal, Mauss decided to pursue sociology and so to join his uncle Émile in Bordeaux during the fall of 1890, rather than thinking of entering the École normale supérieure. His uncle's success in fact served as an example and helped avoid any resistance on the part of his family. During that summer of 1890, he read and was, as his uncle had been in the 1880s, particularly enticed by the works of Théodule Ribot, *English Psychology*[4] and *German Psychology of To-Day, The Empirical School*[5] in particular.

University studies

Enrolled at the Faculty of Letters to obtain a first diploma, the *licence*, in philosophy, he also studied law for a year, from 1891 to 1892. The following year, he interrupted his studies to perform his military service and returned to his native region, to Neufchâteau, where he was assigned to the non-combatant services.[6]

Durkheim would play for him not only the role of a kindly, vigilant guardian, guiding him in his studies and helping him organize his life, but also that of mentor. Through the power of his intellect and his moral ideals, he became a model for his nephew. Mauss' philosophical training was nevertheless open to psychology and sociology and, other than Durkheim, the professors who had a profound intellectual influence on him were Alfred Espinas and Octave Hamelin. After receiving the *licence ès lettres*, he decided to prepare for the *agrégation* competition in philosophy in Paris, and during that time lived with his cousin Albert Cahen, who was a medical student at the time.[7]

While attending classes and lectures at the Sorbonne to prepare for the *agrégation*, Mauss frequented the student socialist political milieu, joined the French Worker's Party and would remain politically active from that time on. As a delegate of the Collectivist Student Group to various congresses of the socialist and cooperative movement, he was the personification of the alliance of intellectual workers and manual workers. In addition, violently opposed to the intellectual dictatorship imposed by the bourgeoisie, he wished to develop a social consciousness in students and teachers, notably by actively participating in an international journal of economics, history and philosophy, *Le Devenir social* (Social Change), founded in 1895.[8]

At the Sorbonne, he met some of his future friends: Edgar Milhaud, Abel Rey and Paul Fauconnet; their common professors were Émile Boutroux, Gabriel Séailles and Victor Brochard. Together they attended Ribot's classes at the Collège de France.[9]

Mauss placed third in the *agrégation* competition.[10]

Already interested for some years in the study of religions, he then planned to prepare a doctoral thesis on the study of "oral ritual and religious ideation",[11] which necessarily led him to complete his education. This is why, beginning in the fall of 1895, as a scholarship student, he opted for the École pratique des hautes études, where he enrolled in the Fourth section of historical sciences and philology and in the Fifth section of religious sciences. Mauss very quickly decided to meet Sylvain Lévi (1863–1935), a professor of Sanskrit and East Indian religions, but also unquestionably France's leading orientalist. Abel Berdaigne's favourite student, Lévi prepared his *Doctrine du sacrifice dans les Brahmanas* (1898) for publication.[12]

Mauss' interests and preoccupations revolved around, on the one hand, the study of languages (Indo-European comparative linguistics with Antoine Meillet, Sanskrit with Louis Finot, Hebrew with Israël Lévi) and, on the other,

44 Mauss

the study of religions (the ancient religions of India, with Sylvain Lévi and Alfred Foucher, and primitive religions with Léon Marillier, whose critical method of ethnographic facts Mauss would in particular adopt).[13]

While they all became mentors for Mauss, Sylvain Lévi very quickly became "his second uncle" and a model with whom he immediately established a father–son relationship, and which over the years transformed into steadfast friendship. Mauss was able to benefit from not only his advice but also his support. In particular, Lévi advised him to spend time studying in the Netherlands and Great Britain in 1897–1898, something which would inspire him to undertake work on sacrifice. They would meet regularly to discuss their respective writings, academic strategies and various different questions.[14]

Certain of the students of this School – namely Henri Hubert, Henri Beuchat, Arnold Van Gennep, Paul Fauconnet, Daniel Halévy and Isidore Lévy, along with two English-speaking colleagues, Joe Stickney and Mabel Bode – became Mauss' friends or collaborators. Thus, Mauss met Hubert in 1896, and they became, as he said, "work twins" or "Siamese twins", although they pursued different social and scholarly paths.[15] The first study they undertook together was for *L'Année sociologique*. It was a matter of "Essay on the Nature and Function of Sacrifice".

Mauss' father and his uncle Émile's father both died in the course of 1896.

Writings and activities between 1895 and 1900

Between 1895 and 1900, Mauss multiplied his academic, research and publishing activities. Indeed, while pursuing his studies of the history of religions and writing his first book reviews, in spite of his slowness and tardiness, he became a genuine research assistant and a valuable collaborator for his uncle. Thus, when he was writing *Suicide*, Durkheim again asked his nephew to reread the manuscript, establish the indispensable bibliographical references and finalise the last statistical tables. Before he had even finished his training at the École pratique, Mauss had thus published his first writings, which were book reviews submitted, notably in 1896, to the prestigious *Revue de l'histoire des religions*, the first of which was about a book by Adolf Bastian. In addition, when he decided to undertake scholarly work in the Netherlands and England in 1897–1898, he was concerned about examining the state of religious science and wished to meet scholars and professors such as H. Kern, C. P. Tiele and Oort in Leiden, Willem Caland in Breda and Tylor and Moritz Winternitz in Oxford. He considered it necessary to make the British anthropological school and its representatives (notably James Frazer, Andrew Lang and E. Sidney Hartland) known in France as a particularly important intellectual movement.[16]

During this period, Mauss also played a major role in the creation and preparation of the first issue of *L'Année sociologique*, in particular as Durkheim's Paris recruiter from 1895 to 1902. In addition, he would indicate and affirm to his collaborators, Durkheim above all, the prime importance of ethnography for sociology. It was for the second volume of *L'Année sociologique* that Mauss and Hubert undertook their first major study on sacrifice (1899), which had a deliberately polemical side because they criticised different renowned figures. Setting aside any history and any genesis of sacrifice, the authors focussed their comparative analysis on two different religions, Hinduism and Judaism, with a view to arriving at sufficiently general conclusions. It was in fact a matter of conferring a social function and dimension upon religion.[17]

The professor–researcher at the École pratique, but also the socialist

At the end of his stay abroad, Mauss found himself facing the same problem regarding what his professional future would be.

In 1900, he accepted temporary teaching responsibilities at the École pratique. It was a matter of teaching about the religions of India, replacing Foucher. Then, upon the death of Sabatier in April 1901 and Marillier in October 1901, Hubert and Mauss would apply for their positions and be accepted. Thus, in 1901, Mauss succeeded Marillier as the holder of the chair of history of the religions of uncivilised peoples and from then on pursued in a career as a professor–researcher.[18]

During this first year, 1901–1902, around fifteen students were enrolled in his seminar on studies of the elementary forms of prayer and on the critical study of documents about magic among the Melanesians. The year 1902–1903 would be marked by the publication of *A General Theory of Magic*, in collaboration with Hubert.[19] Hubert and Mauss were in fact animated by a desire to understand the institutions and wanted to demonstrate that sacrifice and magic were social phenomena. Then, in 1904–1905, Mauss and Beuchat wrote *Essai sur les variations saisonnières des sociétés Eskimos. Etude de morphologie sociale.*[20]

In the political realm, the socialist movement was in complete turmoil, and, after the fashion of many young intellectuals, Mauss became swept up in socialist action. He became involved in numerous ways: through the organisation of courses in groups of socialist students, so as to give socialism orators, lecturers and writers; through playing an active role in the new *Fédération des Jeunesses Socialistes Révolutionnaires*; through his participation in meetings and congresses of the socialist and cooperative movement; through lectures; and also through articles published in *Le Mouvement Socialiste* and in *L'Humanité*, a newspaper created by Jean Jaurès, the first issue of which appeared on April 18, 1904. He had a lively desire to contribute to the emergence of unified socialism, represented by Jaurès who was hostile to the intransigence of the followers of Jules Guesde.[21]

In July 1906, the Ministry of Public Education accorded Mauss a free mission in Russia for the purpose of engaging in ethnographic research there. Then, in 1907, the death of Albert Réville, who held the chair of the history of religions at the Collège de France, afforded the then 35-year-old Mauss an opportunity to apply for it; he held out the hope of transforming the chair into a chair

46 Mauss

of sociology. Though supported by Levi, Janet and Meillet in particular, his candidacy failed.[22]

From the failure of his candidacy at the Collège de France to the beginning of World War I

Then involved in his research into prayer, Mauss did not work on any new significant writings, and the publication of *L'Année sociologique* was still over-burdening him with work. Moreover, he was strengthening his relationships with English anthropologists, who showed great respect for him, and decided to return to England at the beginning of summer 1912 within the framework of a mission that also took him to Belgium and Germany. Its aim was twofold: on the one hand, to consult documentation on Australian tribes and, on the other hand, to explore various different institutions devoted to ethnography, which was flourishing much more there than in France.

In London, he worked at the British Museum every day; familiarised himself with the Australian writings of Alfred Reginald Radcliffe-Brown, with whom he began to correspond; met Charles Gabriel Seligman, who would become a future friend; and then met William Halse Rivers Rivers, Alfred Cort Haddon in Cambridge and Robert Ranulph Marett in Oxford.[23]

In addition, Mauss became increasingly interested in ethnography, defined as the "description of so-called primitive peoples", a discipline which had experienced a "true eclipse" in France and the present development of which was stagnant and therefore very worrisome, unlike in English-speaking countries. Mauss also displayed a great deal of interest in ethnographic museology and began to prepare questionnaires which became guides to research in the field. Furthermore, some of his students were engaging in fieldwork: Marius Barbeau in Canada, Claude Maître in Indonesia and René Maunier in Egypt.

But Mauss also *took care to convince his interlocutors of the usefulness of what is called descriptive sociology for colonists and administrators of colonies.* It is this sociology that he developed within the French school of sociology led by Durkheim.[24]

World War I

Even though he did not make peace an "exclusive goal", Mauss was a pacifist and internationalist. Germany having declared war on Russia and France, Mauss wanted to enlist, even though he had recently been appointed assistant director of studies at the École pratique. He therefore left on September 3 as a volunteer for the whole length of the war. On December 15, he was assigned as an interpreter to a combat unit, the 27th British division, and had to go to Le Havre. He would say that he felt fine. In February 1916, he learned of the death of his cousin, André Durkheim, killed in Serbia, and then in November 1917 that of his uncle. The war was a terrible ordeal for him.[25]

The legacy of Durkheim and his scientific and political concerns

Back in Paris, Mauss returned to his apartment and his place at the École pratique, where he postponed the beginning of his classes until 1919–1920.

Durkheim having died, Mauss was henceforth the custodian of his thought and method. His uncle's numerous unpublished writings represented an enormous burden for his nephew, who not only felt duty-bound to defend his work but also to make it known to the public. Mauss strove, notably, to publish the course devoted to the history of socialism that his uncle had taught in Bordeaux from November 1895 to May 1896. As for *L'Année sociologique,* some attempts to revive it were made at the beginning of 1921, which would finally lead to the publication of a new series starting in 1925, the year during which Mauss presented his essay *The Gift,*[26] which was notably inspired by some of Ribot's ideas in *The Psychology of the Emotions.*[27] In addition, in June 1923 those mainly in charge of the journal founded the Institut français de sociologie (IFS), over which Mauss would preside.[28]

Nevertheless, from the beginning of the 1920s, a time of socio-economic and political upheaval, the projects Mauss developed were inseparably intellectual and political and would display his loyalty to both Jaurès' political notions and the scientific methods founded by his uncle.[29]

Shortly after the signing of the Treaty of Versailles, around the end of 1919 or early 1920, he first entertained the project of undertaking a major work on the nation, the beginnings of which he presented in a talk in Oxford in 1920 called "The Problem of Nationality". This was a time when the principle of nationalities was triumphing and the life of nations was actually becoming an object of reflection, not only for political activists, but also for specialists in the human sciences. He also planned to write a book on bolshevism, for which he prepared an outline.[30]

Regarding his relations with psychologists and psychology, Mauss had never before followed their work so attentively, and he recognized the considerable progress made by this discipline over the course of the last years, even to the point of participating in the activities of the Société de psychologie and accepting to be its president in 1923. He considered Charles Blondel and Georges Dumas to be "our" friends and also counted among them Ignace Meyerson, assistant editor of the *Journal de psychologie normale et pathologique.* In 1924, he gave his famous lecture on the "Real and Practical Relations between Psychology and Sociology",[31] which I shall return to at a later point.

In addition, Mauss followed with a great deal of interest the writings of his friend and anthropologist Seligman, who, along with Rivers, was one of the finest field anthropologists of his generation in Great Britain. [32]

In December 1925, Mauss, Paul Rivet and Lucien Lévy-Bruhl created the Institut d'ethnologie de Paris, which opened its doors at the very beginning of 1926.[33] I shall have more to say about his role in the blossoming of French ethnology later on.

48 Mauss

Hubert died on May 25, 1927. Mauss would also become the "custodian" of his spiritual brother's thought after thirty years of fraternal collaboration.[34]

Mauss' appointment to the Collège de France

Mauss' influence was at that point international, and despite his failure in 1907, he applied again for a position at the Collège de France in 1930 following the death of Jean Izoulet. His mother died at the age of 82 on the eve of the decisive session on November 29, 1930, and on February 3, 1931, the President of France named him to the chair of sociology, replacing Jean Izoulet. He gave his inaugural lecture on February 23, 1931, then taught a first series of courses from 1931 to 1940. His project consisted of pursuing his comparative studies while staying on the fringes of several sciences – sociology, anthropology, psychology and philosophy – although he remained attached to the history of religions of so-called primitive peoples and to ethnology.[35]

From 1931 to World War II: national and international recognition

During these years, Mauss divided his time between teaching; the long labour involved in editing Hubert's books *The Rise of the Celts* and *The Greatness and Decline of the Celts*;[36] and his personal writings, which remained too dispersed and very often fragmentary, something which he recognized and lamented.[37]

So, what about the Durkheimian sociology of which Mauss was the heir and custodian, as well as the movement of Durkheimian sociologists of which he was the leader?

The idea of sociology made inroads at the turn of the 1930s, and Durkheimians consolidated their position in the university system. But there was a "palpable uneasiness", owing to a limited number of chairs in the faculties, a lack of consensus about the definition of the discipline and a lack of interest in sociological theory. Sociology was going through a difficult period. There was a problem of finding successors. A generation had been decimated by World War I. Young people were excessively interested in politics. Moreover, the general situation marked by the economic crisis called for reorientation. Sociology needed to abandon the realm of ideas for that of facts and to develop the purely descriptive side of the social sciences.[38]

The main gathering place of Durkheimians was the Institut français de sociologie. They did not alone represent all of French sociology or everything that counted in French sociology, but they were persuaded that they were practicing the true sociology in France, even if Durkheim was still an object of lively criticism. In 1933, there was talk of reviving the journal in the form of *Annales sociologiques*, and new collaborators appeared on the scene, among them Raymond Aron and Jean Stoetzel. The Durkheimians controlled the field of sociology at both the Sorbonne and the Collège de France, and with the *Annales sociologiques* they had the means of keeping the Durkheimian tradition alive. But they had to face a considerable challenge: that of giving their discipline a distinctly more empirical orientation open to dealing with social problems, and of professionalising it, as had been done in the United States. And Mauss had to accord priority to involvement in that urgent project. It should further be stated that the Durkheimians continued to be the representatives of French sociology in other countries.[39]

In February 1938, Mauss was elected president of the section of religious sciences at the École pratique, a responsibility he accepted without enthusiasm. His prestige was international then, notably in the United States, where his work was known and appreciated. An anglophile, he was undeniably, as he claimed, "one of the French sociologists and anthropologists in closest contact with the English school of anthropology". He was linked by strong bonds of friendship to Charles and Brenda Seligman, as well as to the Frazers. Finally, when Malinowski lectured at the Institut d'ethnologie, he hoped that Mauss would be able to attend.[40]

During those years, he also suffered to a certain extent due to health problems, on the one hand – his own (a slight facial paralysis) and those of his wife – and to growing loneliness connected with the death of colleagues and close friends (Simiand, Sylvain Lévi and Meillet). Finally, he had to bear up under very heavy teaching and administrative responsibilities and the divisions of the SFIO, the French branch of the workers' Internationale, with the rise of fascism looming in the background.

World War II

France and Great Britain declared war on Germany in September 1939, and that autumn Mauss chose leave his professorship at the École pratique in order to retire. Then came the defeat of French armies and the occupation of Paris by German troops, and Pétain, named President of the Council, moved his government to Vichy. He enacted various different repressive measures, and anti-Semitism raged tragically. Soon, in 1942, Jews were obliged to wear the yellow Star of David. During the autumn of 1940, Mauss requested authorisation to resign his position as president of the Fifth section of the École pratique. His life in Paris became precarious and his administrative and scientific activities were quite restricted. In August 1942, he was evicted from his big apartment, which had been requisitioned for a German general, and had to move into a very small ground floor apartment, which quickly became "impracticable".[41]

His final years

Paris was liberated at the end of August 1944, and Mauss then sought to reclaim his apartment on Boulevard Jourdan and resume his work. He was again very sought after. He became professor emeritus at the Collège de France starting on February 23, 1945.

50 Mauss

Following the war, three initiatives marked the revival of French sociology, and those responsible for them wished to associate Mauss with them. These were the creation of the Centre d'études sociologiques and of the *Cahiers internationaux de sociologie* in 1946 and the revival of *L'Année sociologique* in 1949. One of the first colloquia organised by the new centre was on "Mauss and the Social Sciences", in homage to him. But his friends, disciples and collaborators were saddened to see him in such a diminished state.

Sick and bedridden, his wife Marthe died on August 1, 1947, while Mauss, stricken with bronchitis, died on February 11, 1950, at the age of 77.[42]

His creation: transforming–developing Durkheimian sociology

The complexity of social facts

Mauss had an abiding sense of the complexity of reality, of facts, of diversity, of differences, of interweavings and of networks. He considered science to be a strict, inductive discipline based on facts, which are in endless supply. Points of view on reality, these are interdependent and form complex totalities. This principle of the interdependence of social facts, also discovered by historians through their analytical practices, would be a sociological postulate founding the sociological method.

In his essay "Divisions et proportions des divisions en sociologie" (1927), Mauss identified two characteristics distinguishing every social fact from the facts of individual psychology:

1. *It is statistical and numerical*, being common to specific numbers of people during specific periods of time;
2. It is *historical*, because regarding this latter indicator, one must specify that every social fact is a moment in the history of a group of human beings; it is the end and beginning of several series. Simply put, therefore, any social fact, including acts of consciousness, is a fact of life. The term physiology is comprehensive.[43]

Mauss validated the division of social phenomena established by Durkheim, which he considered comprehensive, complete and concrete, not dividing anything that was not already divided in reality and therefore realistic, because it presents us with reality all at once. What sociologists must in fact describe, what is given at each instant, is a "social whole" integrating individuals who are themselves "wholes".

Finally, Mauss accorded methodological value to the monograph, resulting from this principle of the interdependence of social facts and the specific nature of each society, which would lead him to the idea of the total social fact.

Pluralism or methodological eclecticism

From this perspective, he recognised and necessarily adopted a veritable pluralism of methods which he nevertheless intended to reconcile with a certain pragmatism, the whole combining with the principle of the unity of social science which would take shape in an *anthropology*. He would in fact orient Durkheimian sociology, but also ethnography and anthropology, towards a model other than that of biology, so dear to Durkheim, which he would seek in the practice of comparative history, of textual criticism, of philology and linguistics.

Moreover, he considered that sociology could not be constituted outside of ethnography and history, major reservoirs of facts. But, in return, he also introduced the necessary "sociological method" into the field of ethnography itself, something to which Durkheim would subscribe. Indeed, beginning in 1898, Mauss would criticise this school vigorously, and through it the anthropology of his time in an article he wrote for the first issue of *L'Année sociologique* on the English school of anthropology and the theory of religion according to Jevons.

There he wrote that explanation, like all the explanations of anthropology, consists of discovering the psychic core of the whole of humanity amid the variety of phenomena. Then, he went on to say that anthropology was a vague, imprecise science in which comparison is not governed by rigorous canons, where the search for conflicting facts is in no way of prime importance and the study of concordances is everything, with the study of differences secondary. The reason for this is that anthropology is a branch of individual psychology. The method of comparative religion is therefore of the same nature. It is always a matter of discovering the individual mental processes at the basis of facts: beliefs or religious acts. The discovery of psychic principles exhausts the search and explanation. When one has compared the rules of taboo and the laws of the association of ideas, when one has correlated the origin of religions and magic with a primitive notion of causality, the goal has been attained. A certain intellectualism is the hidden principle behind this method. The actions of human beings are supposed to depend on their worldviews. It is not in terms of social needs or in terms of social institutions that the form of religious phenomena is explained, but in terms of completely individual conceptions.[44]

He thus considered that their socio-cultural facts were constructed in a way that made them imprecise, insufficiently criticised and taken out of their social context. Moreover, their interpretation—explanation always consisted of discovering the individual mental processes one believed to be at the basis of social facts. Finally, their mode of reconstructing the past led them to recount a history unattested to by any document.

In short, his methodological eclecticism consisted of fruitful interaction among sociology, ethnology and history, with which he would also associate religious science and philology; each one, however, remains separate and differentiated from the others, all the while working together, facts permitting. No science can replace another.

52 Mauss

In addition, he integrated psychology and linguistics into the field of sociology, thus effecting, as Karsenti has noted, a veritable epistemological displacement of the sociological project. Indeed, unlike Durkheim, Mauss tended to favour an *expressive logic*, support for which was to be sought in the combined input of psychology and linguistics.

Karsenti reminds us that at the time Mauss developed his conceptions, linguists such as Antoine Meillet still bowed to the authority of sociologists, Durkheimians in particular. But this progressive centrality of linguistics would change the internal balance of the social and human sciences and enable the former, according to Mauss, to "separate themselves" from philosophy. Karsenti has stressed that it alone provided a model of scientificity which, correctly applied in the sociological domain, at the same time had a purifying effect, entailing the definitive rejection of conceptual abstractions and teleological reasoning.[45]

So, the affirmation of linguistic domination from the 1920s on can be understood as finally giving the social and human sciences access to the exact sciences. In addition, Mauss made sociology conscious of the fact that its object only genuinely takes shape if integrated into a *system comparable to that of language*.[46] Let us not forget that this is not a matter of Saussurian linguistics, with which Mauss did not seem to be familiar. Through the fact itself, this linguistic model, having become central and significant, leads to an understanding of the social as a language apt to be expressed in distinct instances, all the while preserving its unity, just as it must essentially be conceived of as a certain *system of meaning*.

Finally, Mauss could thus envisage a new relationship between the individual and the social: no longer conceived of as two antagonistic dimensions, as for Durkheim, but in a *relationship of translation*, one acquiring a meaning for the other. According to Tarot, this notion of translation had to serve to recapture the in-depth complexity of the levels signifying the real, just as it had to allow their articulation. They all offer limited views of a totality upon which they are interdependent because they are seen interacting with one another, so that there is always transformation in going from one level to the other. And the translation presupposes a transformation into another system, different from the preceding one.

As for the *collective psychology* introduced by Mauss, followed by his Durkheimian colleague Maurice Halbwachs and validated by the psychologist Charles Blondel, it anticipated the development of French sociological thought and began to receive recognition in France during the interwar period. Sociological in nature, it is riveted to the "physio-morphological" pole, that is, it only constitutes its own object by relating to real movements and forms of the group studied, integrating the three factors: morphological, statistic and historical. This is why it is specific and irreducible to the collective psychology – that of Mac Dougall in particular – consisting only of the study of "individual interactions" taken out of their social substrate, which began to develop during the 1920s in England and the United States.

The creation of modern French ethnology

Creation of the Institut d'ethnologie and the rapid expansion of French ethnology

In the face of the catastrophic reality of the situation of French ethnography and the urgent nature of the measures to be put into place, a little before World War I, Mauss submitted to the Minister of Public Education a project for the creation of a "bureau, institute or department of ethnology", strictly scientific in nature, gathering specialists from different parts of the world. Attached to the university system and not to a ministry, as in other countries, it would have an autonomous organisation and scientific personnel. In addition, with priority given to practicing ethnography, explorations in Oceania, Asia and Africa would have to be organised very quickly. Teaching would come in a second phase.

It must be explained that up until then, in Paris, the teaching of anthropology and anthropological research were located in the following different institutions: l'École d'anthropologie, the chairs of anthropology of the Museum d'Histoire Naturelle, those of the religions of uncivilised peoples at the École pratique and the École of prehistory at the Collège de France, the Institut de paléontologie humaine, the Musée d'Ethnographie at Trocadero, the École coloniale and the École des langages orientales vivantes.

Mauss' wish would finally be granted when the Institut d'ethnologie was officially created in December 1925 within the context of the May 1924 political victory of the "Cartel des gauches", a union of the radical Left, the socialist republicans and the socialists (SFIO). It would be directed by academics identified with the SFIO. Located in the building of the Institut de géographie, it opened its doors at the very beginning of 1926. Its directorship reflected the three tendencies in French ethnology as represented by Mauss (École pratique des hautes études), Paul Rivet (Museum d'histoire naturelle) and Lucien Lévy-Bruhl (the Sorbonne).[47]

Originally financed by the general governments and those of the colonies, the Institute would have a twofold mission: that of training professional ethnologists who would contribute to the progress of ethnological science, but also that of teaching all those living or destined to live in the colonies and who, be they administrators, missionaries, physicians or military men, were often in a position to make good ethnographical observations and consequently *"to place the results of that science in the hands of our native policy whenever asked"*[48] (my emphasis).

Ethnology then underwent rapid expansion during the 1920s and 1930s. To first generations of students that Mauss had trained before World War I, among whom he had recruited several collaborators of *L'Année sociologique*, were added new students, several of whom pursued a career in ethnography or in ethnology

54 Mauss

and would become major French figures. Thus, in the 1920s, the following may be named in particular: Jeanne Cuisinier, Georges Dumézil, Marcel Griaule, Alexandre Koyré, Alfred Métraux, Georges-Henri Rivière, André Varagnac. Figuring in the 1930s were: Roger Caillois, Germaine Dieterlen, Louis Dumont, André-Georges Haudricourt, Maurice Leenhardt, Michel Leiris, André Leroi-Gourhan, Denise Paulme, André Schaeffner, Jacques Soustelle, Germaine Tillion, Jean-Pierre Vernant, Paul-Émile Victor.

This group of students was obviously heterogeneous in terms of age, nationality, training and professional orientation, and the number of young women was relatively high.[49]

As the master of French ethnology, even those who were not Mauss' students requested to see him and ask his advice. This was the case with Roger Bastide, Jacques Berque and Claude Lévi-Strauss, who, very interested in ethnology, wrote to Mauss to ask him for advice and orientation as soon as he had the *agrégation* in philosophy.

The Institut d'ethnologie prospered during the late 1920s and the early 1930s. Indeed, Mauss taught. His students left to do their first work in the field and prepare their theses. The late 1930s, a prosperous period, were marked by the opening of the Musée de l'Homme and the Musée des Arts et Traditions populaires and then by the multiplication of missions (the Trans-Greenland expedition, Sahara-Cameroun, Djebel-Aurès, missions of Lévi-Strauss in Brazil, of Leroi-Gourhan in Japan, of Cuisinier-Delmas in Indochina). The new Musée de l'Homme made a genuine research laboratory available to ethnologists, while the Institut d'ethnologie moved into the Palais de Chaillot and continued its work of training future professional ethnologists and colonial administrators.[50]

Aspects of his teaching based on the Manuel d'ethnographie

In his course, published in 1926 under the title *Manuel d'ethnographie* by Denise Paulme, one of his students,[51] Mauss envisaged responding above all to questions of a practical nature and learning "to observe and classify" social phenomena, the field of which was limited to the indigenous societies peopling the French colonies, but also to other societies "at the same stage". He thus offered "necessary instructions" for scientifically constituting their archives. He explained that they were also addressed to administrators and colonists lacking professional training. It was a matter of instructions for "clearing the way" so as to enable them to accomplish work intermediary between an extensive and an intensive study of the population under consideration.

According to Mauss, the aim of ethnological science, a "science of observations and statistics", was the observation of societies, and its goal knowledge of social facts, which are first and foremost historical and therefore irreversible. It thus included a historical dimension, which would consist of establishing the history of human populations, while comparative ethnography had to be founded on comparisons of facts and not of cultures.

All ethnographers would have to take care to be exact and complete. They had to have a sense of the facts and of their interrelationships, a sense of proportions and articulations.[52] However, they would encounter inevitable difficulties during their investigations, from which he distinguished two types of methods: extensive and intensive.

The extensive method consists of seeing the greatest number of people as possible in a specific area and time. It often enables one to locate a place where intensive work can be carried out at a later point. But it is inevitably superficial. Of course, professional ethnographers must preferably practice the intensive method consisting of the complete, in-depth observation of a tribe, realisable over a period of three or four years.

They arbitrarily divide methods of observation into: on the one hand, material methods of recording and observing (morphological and cartographic, statistical, geographic and demographic, photographic and phonographic methods); and, on the other hand, methods of observing and recording (philological, sociological and interrogatory methods), all the while knowing that in social life, there is neither any pure material element, nor any pure psychological element.

His plan for studying any society involved three fundamental sectors:

Social morphology, which includes demography, human geography and technomorphology, or the set of relationships between the technical resources and the geographical basis or ground of social life. He in fact set down as a methodological rule that social life, in all its forms – for example, moral, religious, juridical and economic – was a function of its material substrate, and that social life varies with this substrate, meaning with the mass, the density, the form and the composition of the human groupings. He demonstrated this in his *Essai sur les variations saisonnières des sociétés Eskimos. Etude de morphologie sociale,* co-authored with Henri Beuchat in 1904–1905.

Physiology, which includes the following domains: technology, aesthetics, economy, law, religion and sciences, notably.

General phenomena, be they linguistic, national or international, but also what he called collective ethology.

Methodological and epistemological characteristics of Maussian ethnology

Let us begin with the observation that the Maussian ethnography–ethnology established after World War I is in line with, and bears witness to, that period of profound crisis for science and western reason, whose founding beliefs, be they a matter of determinism, indefinite progress, liberation and happiness through rationalisation or the superiority of western civilisation, had been challenged, even shaken.

It represented privileged access to human complexity, the expression of which goes by way of symbolic systems. Moreover, it constituted an ideal terrain for exercising his methodological pluralism, as described above. He was in fact able

56 Mauss

to combine methods of historical criticism that enabled him to effect a critical examination of the ethnographic literature with the Durkheimian sociological method, but also with the philological method which would confer the sense of detail as well as that of the whole. In so doing, thanks to the philological method, ethnography could reintegrate language and with it, the way societies view themselves. Thus, according to Mauss, ethnologists must simultaneously look at wholes and contexts and at details, none of which should be neglected, since one can never judge importance and place in the whole in advance. One must also seek to connect the whole and the part, a principle of the Durkheimian method. The purpose of ethnography consists of preserving a material image of the life of societies and, notably, of making the treasure of their oral archives in written archives.

Additionally, Mauss observed that, though different, those societies, like our own, are determined by the principle of *modality*. He in fact considered all social phenomena to be the product of collective will and therefore of a choice between different possible options. They all had a type, a mode, a form, both common and chosen by the collectivity from among other possible forms. That is why the domain of the social is that of *modality*. And since there is not an infinite number of these possible options, there are therefore limits to arbitrariness.

Ultimately, according to Tarot (1999), Mauss' contribution to ethnography is without a doubt to be summed up in this precept: *find the point of view of the indigenous person*, which comes down, on the one hand, to recognizing that he or she has one and, on the other hand, giving him or her an opportunity to speak, because this gives privileged access to that point of view. In this re-evaluation of the point of view and words of indigenous peoples, he is expressly referring to the practices of American ethnology. It is first a matter of a problem of ethnographic methodology and of a general principle of field ethnography that "only the indigenous point of view counts". In the history of ethnology, this is recognizing that each society has the right to speak about itself, just as each person does about his or her society, something which ethnocentrism and western rationalism had often denied them.

The whole person: a figure unifying anthropological knowledge

Mauss considered that in sociology of representations and practices, as in collective psychology, we encounter a human being in his or her totality, with his or her body, mentality and society given all at once in one fell swoop. Everything is mixed together there. Consequently, we are dealing with facts of a very complex kind, which he proposed calling "phenomena of totality",[53] referring to a common object of study, that of the complete human being, which seemed to him to be among the urgent things to explore.

Thus, according Karsenti in *L'homme total*, Mauss replaced the Durkheimian epistemological figure of the *homo duplex* – split in two by the dividing line between the individual and the social correlative to the unbridgeable gap between the sciences of the social (sociology, ethnology and history) and the sciences of the individual (psychology and physiology) – with an epistemological figure which was both unified and differentiated, designated by the *whole person*, three-dimensional (biological, psychological and sociological) and constituted of multiple connexions and relationships. A complete, concrete object, this figure is both totally individual and totally social, and this unified totality can be apprehended on three levels as distinct as they are interdependent.

Consequently, by thus becoming a unified figure of knowledge, this whole person requires, to Karsenti's mind, a complete reformulation of the ties connecting psychology, biology and sociology and therefore a profound modification of the interdisciplinary relationships among the sciences of human beings. In so doing, these were determined to be conceived from then on as the interdependent parts of a complete anthropology, realised then solely in virtue of their actual collaboration.[54]

Ethnology after Mauss, henceforth dubbed "the father of modern anthropology"

French ethnology, then provided with much more solid institutional base – including in particular the Musée de l'Homme and that of Arts et traditions populaires, the Fifth and Sixth sections of the École pratique and the Centre National de la recherche scientifique – would be able to continue to evolve and thrive owing to the momentum imparted to the teaching and diverse domains of research initiated and developed by Mauss.

Leenhardt would take over the chair of the history of the religions of uncivilised peoples, which he would leave in 1951, while Georges Gurvitch in sociology and Claude Lévi-Strauss in anthropology would perpetuate, each in his own way, the master's teaching.

Mauss consequently acquired the status of "father of modern anthropology" but just of "precursor" in sociology, thus losing that of "head of a school". The sociologists would in fact leave Mauss to the anthropologists, who would themselves forget him somewhat. In addition, the very title of the anthology presented by Lévi-Strauss, *Sociology and anthropology*, would soon appear outdated because it no longer seemed possible for the two disciplines to exist side by side.

As for Lévi-Strauss, he would replace Leenhardt at the École pratique in 1951, and the chair would come to be that of the comparative religions of peoples without writing. Assistant Director of the Musée de l'Homme, he had just published his thesis *The Elementary Structures of Kinship* (1949),[55] but had also just launched a journal, *L'Homme*, which is a series of journals of ethnology, geography and linguistics. He proved to be Mauss' true successor. Finally, at the time of his entry into Collège de France in 1959, he took the chair of social anthropology. I shall of course come back to Lévi-Strauss in my conclusion. Ten years later, the assembly of professors of the Collège would create a chair of sociology of modern civilisation and elect Raymond Aron, Mauss' young cousin.

58 Mauss

Notes

1 Marcel Fournier, *Marcel Mauss: A Biography*, Princeton NJ, Princeton University Press, 2006 (1994).
2 *Ibid.*, pp. 9–10.
3 *Ibid.*, pp. 11, 16.
4 Théodule Ribot, *English Psychology*, New York, D. Appleton, 1874 (1870).
5 Théodule Ribot, *German Psychology To-Day, The Empirical School*, New York, Charles Scribner's Sons, 1886 (1870).
6 *Op. cit.*, Fournier, *Marcel Mauss: A Biography*, pp. 20–21.
7 *Ibid.*, pp. 21, 23–24, 28.
8 *Ibid.*, p. 34.
9 *Ibid.*, p. 30.
10 *Ibid.*, p. 31.
11 *Ibid.*, p. 32.
12 *Ibid.*, pp. 37, 40, 44.
13 *Ibid.*, p. 44.
14 *Ibid.*, pp. 47–48.
15 *Ibid.*, pp. 44, 48.
16 *Ibid.*, pp. 53, 56, 58.
17 *Ibid.*, pp. 64, 75.
18 *Ibid.*, pp. 85–88.
19 Marcel Mauss, *A General Theory of Magic*, London, Routledge, 1972 (1902).
20 *Op. cit.*, Fournier, *Marcel Mauss: A Biography*, pp. 92–93.
21 *Ibid.*, pp. 100–104.
22 *Ibid.*, pp. 129, 150.
23 *Ibid.*, p. 164.
24 *Ibid.*, p. 166.
25 *Ibid.*, pp. 168, 174, 175, 178, 182.
26 Marcel Mauss, *The Gift: The Form and Reason for Exchange in Archaic Societies*, London, Routledge, 1990 (1925).
27 Théodule Ribot, *The Psychology of the Emotions*, London, Walter Scott Ltd., 1897.
28 *Op. cit.*, Fournier, *Marcel Mauss: A Biography*, pp. 189, 229.
29 *Ibid.*, pp. 189, 204.
30 *Ibid.*, pp. 189–191.
31 Marcel Mauss, "Real and Practical Relations between Psychology and Sociology", in *Sociologie and Psychology, Essays Marcel Mauss*, London, Routledge and Kegan Paul, 1979 (1924).
32 *Op. cit.*, Fournier, *Marcel Mauss: A Biography*, p. 223.
33 *Ibid.*, p. 235.
34 *Ibid.*, p. 253.
35 *Ibid.*, pp. 272–273, 276.
36 Henri Hubert, *The Rise of the Celts* and *The Greatness and Decline of the Celts*, first published in English in a single volume entitled *The History of the Celtic People*, London, Kegan Paul, Trench, Trubner, 1934.
37 *Op. cit.*, Fournier, *Marcel Mauss: A Biography*, p. 287.
38 *Ibid.*, pp. 291–292.
39 *Ibid.*, pp. 294, 297, 299.
40 *Ibid.*, pp. 294–95, 318, 320.
41 *Ibid.*, pp. 333, 336, 344–345.
42 *Ibid.*, pp. 348–349.
43 Marcel Mauss, "Divisions et proportions des divisions en sociologie", *L'Année sociologique*, n.s. 2, 1927, reprinted in his *Œuvres*, vol. 3, Paris, Minuit, 1969, pp. 28–29.
44 Marcel Mauss, "L'École anthropologique anglaise et la théorie de la religion selon Jevons", *Œuvres*, vol. 1, 1968, pp. 109–110.

45 *Op. cit.*, Bruno Karsenti, *L'homme total: Sociologie, Anthropologie et Philosophie Chez Marcel Mauss*, Paris, Presses Universitaires de France, 1997, p. 145.
46 *Ibid.*, p. 170, his emphasis.
47 *Op. cit.*, Fournier, *Marcel Mauss: A Biography*, p. 235.
48 *Ibid.*, p. 237.
49 *Ibid.*, p. 404, n. 18.
50 *Ibid.*, pp. 319–320.
51 Marcel Mauss, *Manuel d'ethnographie*, Denise Paulme (ed.), Paris, Payot & Rivages, 2002 (1926).
52 *Ibid.*, p. 20.
53 *Op. cit.*, Fournier, *Marcel Mauss, A Biography*, p. 240.
54 *Op. cit.*, Karsenti, p. 101.
55 Claude Lévi-Strauss, *The Elementary Structures of Kinship*, Boston MA: Beacon Press, 1969 (1949).

4

SYMBOLS, SYMBOLISM AND SYMBOLISATION

Durkheim, Mauss and Freud discussed symbolism and symbolisation in various different texts which marked different stages of their reflection. So, for each of them, I shall successively present these selected fundamental texts, then formulate some remarks, commentaries and personal reflections accompanied by those of specialists. Finally, I shall open a discussion enabling us to identify similarities and differences among the ideas of the three men, but beyond that, it will be their conceptions and the epistemological approaches proper to their creations which will probably come to the fore.

Durkheim, symbolism and symbolisation

Durkheim already engaged in reflections on symbolism and symbolisation in 1893 in *The Division of Labor in Society*, where law is presented as a symbol of social solidarity, and he would pursue them until 1920 in his "Introduction to Ethics".[1] However, his ideas on the subject found their most mature expression in *Elementary Forms of Religious Life*. I shall therefore follow the chronological evolution of his thought, then formulate some personal reflections and remarks backed up by those of Camille Tarot and Bruno Karsenti.

The texts

Law as symbol of social solidarity (1893)

Durkheim proposed to classify and then compare the various different social bonds or different species of "social solidarity" organising any society, thus drawing inspiration from the approach taken by the 18th century naturalists. However, corresponding as it does to an "internal datum" that eludes us, this

Symbols, symbolism and symbolisation **61**

phenomenon is neither amenable to "exact observation" nor to "measurement" – unlike suicide, which is apprehendable through its rate of occurrence in society. Durkheim therefore replaces it with an "external datum" *symbolising* it, becoming a "visible symbol" through which the internal datum will be indirectly explored. This is the law.[2]

He in fact considered that social relationships are regulated and take on a form defined by custom and the law which, according Durkheim, *symbolise* only one part of social life. So, it is by classifying the different species of law in accordance with the different sanctions attached to them that one will be able to discover, according to him, what different species of social solidarity correspond to them. He then distinguished two major species: the first, with its repressive sanctions, covers all penal law; the second, with merely restitutive sanctions, includes civil law, commercial law, procedural law and administrative or constitutional law.[3]

To what kind of social solidarity does each of these species correspond?

He recognised two kinds of positive solidarities or major currents of social life to which two different types of social structure and two species of individual correspond.[4]

Thus, the social solidarity *symbolised by repressive law*, the breaking of which constitutes the crime which will determine its perpetrator's punishment, arises out of resemblances or similarities of consciousnesses, appreciated and sought after by the members of the society, representing a condition of its cohesion. It is a matter of the "mechanical solidarity" that in fact gives rise to legal rules which, under the threat of repressive measures, impose uniform beliefs and practices upon everyone. Society is then conceived of as a more or less organised set of beliefs and sentiments common to all the members of the group. This is "the collective type".[5]

The social solidarity *symbolised by cooperative law having restitutive sanctions* is produced by the social division of labour, a particular form, according to Durkheim, of the physiological division of labour. He called it "organic solidarity". The division of labour in fact gives rise to legal rules determining the nature and peaceful and regular relationships among the functions divided up, but whose infringement only entails measures of reparation. If it produces solidarity, it is because it also creates among people a whole system of rights and duties binding them to one another in a lasting way.[6]

This society with which we are interdependent is therefore a *system of different, special functions united by defined relationships*. It learns to look upon the members, no longer as things over which it has rights, but as *cooperating members* whom it cannot do without and toward whom it has duties. *The individuals then differ from one another.*[7]

Sanction is a symbol of the feeling of obligation based on the following texts on morality: "Définition du fait moral" (1893); "Leçons sur la morale" (1909); "Introduction to ethics" (1920)

By morality, Durkheim meant any system of sanctioned rules of conduct, the distinctive characteristics of which are first of all obligation, then "desirability".

62 Symbols, symbolism and symbolisation

Morality begins with the attachment to any group whatsoever: the basis of social life itself. In addition, he maintained that if therefore we define the moral rule by the sanction attached to it, we are not considering the feeling of obligation to be a product of the sanction. Rather, it is because the sanction derives from the feeling of obligation that the sanction can be used to symbolise it, and since this symbol has the great advantage of being objective, accessible to observation and even to measurement, it is methodologically wise to prefer it to the thing it represents.[8]

Suicide (1897)

Here, Durkheim particularly discusses the materialisation of social life, of social facts, using material things, therefore using *material props* which attest: on the one hand, to society's need to anchor itself and express itself with material props and, on the other hand, to the exteriority itself of what is social in relation to individuals. Moreover, he proposed a definition of religion which is not yet that of 1912:

> Religion is in a word the system of symbols by means of which society becomes conscious of itself; it is the characteristic way of thinking of collective existence. Here then is a great group of states of mind which would not have originated if individual states of consciousness had not combined, and which result from this union and are superadded to those which derive from individual natures.[9]

A little later on he added that "the above observations apply not only to religion, but to law, morals, customs, political institutions, pedagogical practices, etc., in a word to all forms of collective life".[10]

Thus, already in 1897, Durkheim considered that any society, any "collective existence" constituted through the union of individual consciousnesses, *thinks and expresses itself* through symbols. Consequently, these symbols are instruments of thought and expression of states of mind. The set of symbols then forms a *system*, a collective language, a *symbolism*. In addition, each one of the forms of collective life, religion, law, morals or political institutions is then constituted by a system of symbols.

Consequently, collective life is a vast set of systems of symbols enabling each society to think, express itself and, at the same time, become aware of itself.

These ideas are taken up later in my general reflections.

The Elementary Forms of Religious Life (1912)

Durkheim placed the problem of symbol at the centre of his *Elementary Forms of Religious Life* (1912), as Tarot emphasised in *De Durkheim à Mauss, l'invention du symbolique*, through the totem, a place of the projection of collective force and "clan flag". However, it is also found with respect to rites, assemblies and

Symbols, symbolism and symbolisation **63**

"effervescent groups", just as he introduced and developed a sociological theory of symbolism and symbolisation there.

Let us follow his train of thought.

Totem and totemism

Durkheim considered that a certain number *of impersonal, anonymous forces that the human imagination represents to itself in the form of symbols* – of figures borrowed either from the animal realm, or from the vegetable realm – traverse and animate the universe such as it is conceived by totemism. It is a matter of totems. But only the impersonal force or "totemic principle" that they symbolise is the object of a veritable cult. While being a material force, "the totemic principle" is a moral power which is easily transformed into a divinity in the proper sense of the word. Thus, the totem is above all a symbol which expresses and symbolises two different kinds of things. On the one hand, it is the external and perceptible form of the totemic principle, or god. And on the other hand, it is also the symbol of that particular society called the clan. It is its flag, the distinctive mark of its personality.

So the god of the clan, the totemic principle, can therefore be nothing other than the clan itself, but *objectified* and represented to the imagination in the perceptible form of plant or animal species that serve as totems. The unity of the members derives solely from the fact that they have the same name and the same emblem. And this identity of name serves to imply identity of nature.

This aptitude of a society to set itself up as god or to transform things that are purely secular in nature into sacred things, and therefore into religious thought itself, would proceed, according to Durkheim, from a particular social state of general enthusiasm, from an effervescence, which he went on to explore. Nevertheless, he asked whether religion would not for all that be "the product of a kind of delirium".[11]

Religion, delirium and idealism

> What other name can we give to the burst of emotion in which men find themselves when, as the result of a collective effervescence, they believe that they have been swept up into a world quite different from the one they see? It is the case for the religious beliefs populating the social world with forces, for example.
>
> It is true that religious life cannot reach a certain degree of intensity without involving a psychic exaltation that is in some way akin to delirium.[12]

Indeed, if the word delirium denotes "any state in which the mind adds to immediate sensation and projects its feelings and impressions onto things",[13] then collective representations, which very "often attribute to things properties that are not inherent in any form, or to any extent",[14] can then only be delirious in nature. It follows that the world of the religious, which does not belong to

64 Symbols, symbolism and symbolisation

empirical reality, is a "superimposed" world that is delirious in nature. It is the case for the religious beliefs populating the social world with forces, for example.

Indeed, Durkheim points out that "there is a region of nature in which the formula of idealism is applied nearly to the letter" and there "far more than elsewhere, the idea creates the reality". In addition, "in order to express our own ideas to ourselves, we need to anchor them in material things that symbolize them".[15]

Ideas are therefore "realities" and "forces", and "collective representations are forces even more active and powerful than individual representations".[16]

Ultimately, collective thought – religious thought in particular – expresses itself by combining idealism, the creator of reality, and symbolism; collective representations are not delirious in nature, but form rather a "pseudo-delirium", which is "only a form of this fundamental idealism", in which "the ideas objectified in this way are solidly grounded, not in the material things onto which they are grafted, but in the nature of society"[17]

As for religious forces, they are only objectified collective forces, meaning moral forces made up of ideas and feelings which the spectacle of society awakens in each of the members and which are then projected and objectified by being anchored in the objects, which then become sacred.[18]

The ritual aspects

There are two sides to every cult – one negative, the other positive – which in reality are closely associated and presuppose each other.

The negative cult is a set of rites, the purpose of which is to realise that essential state of separation between sacred beings and profane beings, which all take the form of prohibition, or taboo.

The positive cult is a set of ritual practices, the function of which is to regulate and organise positive and bilateral relations between human beings and religious forces. It involves mimetic, representative or commemorative and expiatory rites and is constituted by the cycle of festivals regularly recurring at fixed periods.

While its purpose is to bring profane subjects into communion with sacred beings, it is also charged with keeping those sacred beings alive, with restoring and regenerating them perpetually. However, since these sacred beings are only the symbolic expression of the society, the cult therefore really periodically does recreate and morally regenerate individuals. Their principle purpose is therefore the moral remaking of the individuals and the community.

An essential characteristic of any kind of religion is its "dynamogenic" quality,[19] which society in fact exerts; it is a preeminent source of moral life upon which the moral life of individuals feeds.

Systematic idealisation is, finally, an essential characteristic of religions, and only human beings have the ability to conceive the ideal and to "add to the real", just as the sacred is added on to the real.

Religion therefore expresses this collective ideal.

Collective representations and symbols

Durkheim relates institutions to the "states of collective consciousness" that he calls collective "representations", falling under the "collective mind"; hence, his conception of social life is essentially composed of these collective representations, *sui generis*, which are also symbols expressing and translating the way society represents itself and thinks of itself and the world surrounding it. Consequently, these symbols change in accordance with what it is.

Symbolism as social language and factor of communion, social unity

On their own, individuals are closed to one another and can only encounter one another and communicate providing they come out of themselves through the intermediary of signs translating their inner states.[20]

> Social life, then, in every aspect and throughout its history, is possible only thanks to a vast body of symbolism. The material emblems, the embodied representations ... are a particular form of that symbolism. But there are many others. Collective feelings can be embodied equally in personalities or formulas: some formulas are flags; some personalities, real or mythic, are symbols.[21]

Generally speaking, collective feeling can only be conscious of itself by anchoring itself in a material object. In this way it partakes of the nature of this object and reciprocally.

Remarks, commentaries and reflections

The Durkheimian symbol

Durkheim tried to explain the formation of symbols by the effects of major gatherings during which groups become effervescent. It is the originary force of the social, energy resulting from the gathering of human beings, which is released in each symbol to constitute them, one by one, and separately, as signifying entities. As a consequence, as a "fixer of social forces", symbols are *dynamogenic*.[22]

Treated as a metaphor, a symbol carries within itself a natural link with the reality it symbolises – social reality, in this case. As Karsenti has emphasised, it is a matter of a "thought of representation", where the link between signifier and signified, or between symbol and symbolised, remains unanimously envisaged as a figurative process of substitution of one reality for another.[23] Penal law symbolises the solidarity, the cohesion based on the conformity of all individual consciousnesses; just as in morals, the sanction is a symbol of the feeling of obligation. Finally, the totem is both the symbol of the principle or totemic god, but also that of the clan, of the society.

66 Symbols, symbolism and symbolisation

Thus, *what is peculiar to the Durkheimian symbol is the association of force and representation.* It always translates a collective affective state.

Moreover, through its "materialization" and "objectification" in the form of a "thing" – the emblem or flag – the Durkheimian symbol makes representable the exteriority of the social, conceived as an external force higher than individuals. It constitutes then, according to Karsenti, a signifying entity for the particular consciousnesses which is only able to fulfil its genuine function by also being integrated psychically as "representation". Consequently, by symbol, the presence of the social to individual consciousnesses is affirmed both as "thing" and as "representation", hence the "two-sidedness" of the Durkheimian symbol, identified by Karsenti, as "thing and idea", "figure and representation". Thus tattooing, a mark of the social printed on the body, confirms the characteristics of exteriority of the social and the objectivity of the symbol.

In addition, Durkheim never takes symbols together, enchained. Unlike Mauss, he disregards what signifiers refer to and networks of significations in order to fasten on to the force invested there.

Symbols also appear as crystallizers and conditions of the durability of social feelings.

On the one hand, collective symbols *presentify* the disappearance of social feelings born in the effervescence of human gatherings which no longer exists. On the other hand, they inscribe them and anchor them in things, people, important persons – real or mythical – so as to keep them always alive, something allowing these collective feelings to become conscious of themselves, partaking then of the nature of this symbolic object and "reciprocally".

Symbols, tools of social communication

Symbols are also tools of social communication enabling individual consciousnesses, which on their own are closed to one another,[24] to meet and exchange through the mediation of these signs external to them; they are therefore social in nature, which then translate and express their inner states. Nonetheless, the symbols also contribute to forming inner states, anchoring them and transmitting them.

However, since they represent the social, Karsenti points out that consciousnesses are "in communion" less through it than they are "in communion" in it, coming out of themselves then to reach this signifying space so that, far from guaranteeing continuity between the individual and the social, socialising through symbols confirms their disjunction. Communion, or "fusion of all individual feelings into a common feeling",[25] can then be realized and the signs expressing them produce a single result, such as a single cry, a single word, a single gesture, informing the individuals that they are in unison and making them aware of their moral unity.

Symbolism is thus a language of a collective kind, an instrument of intersubjective communication and a factor of communion, of social unity.

Symbols, symbolism and symbolisation **67**

Symbols are also instruments of collective thought and expression

As early as *Suicide* (1897), Durkheim declared that every society – "collective existence" constituted by the union of individual consciousness – *thinks and expresses itself* through symbols. Social life is essentially composed of collective representations *sui generis* that *are also symbols* and "states of collective consciousness" coming under the "collective mind", to which institutions such as law, morality and religion, in particular, would relate. There is therefore in Durkheim a confusion, detected by Karsenti, between representation and symbol.

On the basis of the existence of collective representations, Durkheim tried to deduce, according to Tarot, the existence of a collective consciousness in order to localize them there.

These symbols express and translate the manner in which society represents itself and thinks of itself and the world surrounding it. Consequently, they are instruments of collective thought; hence, religion is a system of symbols and therefore a mode of thinking proper to every society or "collective existence". Nevertheless, as instruments, these symbols change in accordance with the evolution of society and its representations.

Symbolism and symbolisation

Durkheim affirmed, on the one hand, the need for symbolism for the very existence of human societies ("Social life is only possible thanks to a vast body of symbolism") and, on the other hand, the existence of a distinctiveness of symbolisms and a need for "emblematism".

In addition, he considered that symbolism comes to remedy a limitation constitutive of particular consciousnesses because, being closed in upon themselves according to a prejudice inherited from classic 19th-century psychology, they prove incapable of establishing a direct relationship among themselves. Let us not forget that symbolism would represent even this social life to particular consciousnesses. In fact, according to Karsenti, Durkheim seemed to discover in symbolism, in an overt form, the psychological process characteristic of the functioning of the collective thought at work in social life. Karsenti considers that by examining it, and for the first time, one consequently draws distinctly nearer to the social in its very psychic density.[26]

Idealism, the "creator of reality", and symbolism

Durkheim also drew attention to the fact that in the social realm, "far more than elsewhere, the idea creates the reality" and that, in addition, "in order to express our own ideas to ourselves we need to anchor them in material things that symbolize them".[27] That is why he considered that collective thought, and religious thought in particular, expresses itself by combining idealism, the "creator of reality", and symbolism.

Consequently, I consider that Durkheim's conception of symbolism is necessarily accompanied by idealism, the "creator of reality", which will therefore take on multiple symbolic

68 Symbols, symbolism and symbolisation

forms. They are two interdependent processes of the creation–recreation of society. They form a functional pair.

Moreover, Durkheim thought that *the fact of symbolisation is both a natural fact and a cultural fact.* It is natural to human beings and therefore necessary, but, being cultural, it is particular to each group, hence the paradox of symbolism. A product of nature in a sense, it is owing to it that human beings rise above nature.[28]

Finally, Tarot emphasises that in rare passages of *Elementary Forms of Religious Life* Durkheim comes to consider that *society and symbolisation happen together, that without symbolisation, there would be no social order; hence, one could conclude that society perhaps does not completely pre-exist symbolisation but is created and stabilised with it.* From then on, symbolisation would be the process by which a group in relationship with the world is created not only by anchoring its representations but also by creating and anchoring them through exchanging them in perceptible forms. From this perspective, the processes of symbolisation and idealisation and the creation of any society are interdependent.

Mauss, symbolism and symbolisation

I shall now present the essential content of three texts marking the evolution of Mauss' thought on this theme: *A General Theory of Magic* (1902–1903); "Real and Practical Relations between Psychology and Sociology" (1924); and, finally, *The Gift: The Form and Reason for Exchange in Archaic Societies* (1924). Then I shall formulate some commentaries, remarks and reflections, once again relying on the ideas of Karsenti and Tarot, but also those of Lévi-Strauss.

The texts

A General Theory of Magic

According to Mauss, magic is a *system* of social facts involving different elements (agents, acts and representations, ideas, beliefs) created and qualified by society. It results only from the functioning of collective life. It has two components: collective affective states and a symbolic language.

The magician's image and powers are produced by opinion. The whole group believes in the effectiveness of the rites, which are "kinds of language" expressing and translating ideas. Magical rites follow the laws of sympathy, meaning that they establish necessary relations thought to exist between things, relations between words and signs and the objects represented.

Magic and religion both seem to derive from a common source. It is a matter of collective affective states (needs, desires, expectations, apprehensions, hopes): generators of illusions. They result from a mixture of the individual's own sentiments with those of society as a whole and, furthermore, represent its primary phenomena.

The magician is conceived of as a "kind of official" vested by society with an authority in which he himself is committed to believe. The magician's belief is a reflection of that of the public since the pretences of the magician are only possible because of public credulity.

"We are therefore correct", Mauss maintained, "in assuming that this collective belief in magic brings us face to face with a unanimous sentiment and a unanimous will found in the community or, in other words, precisely those collective forces which we have been looking for".[29]

Magic superimposes the idea of power or magical force comparable to our notion of mechanical force – which is specifically the cause of magical effects (illness and death, happiness and health, etc.) – on that inseparable idea of a milieu, the spiritual world in which it acts.

As Mauss explained,

> In this mysterious milieu, things no longer happen as they do in our world of the senses. Distance does not prevent contact. Desires and images can be immediately realized. It is the spiritual world and the world of spirits at the same time. Since everything is spiritual, anything may become a spirit. ... things happen according to laws, those inevitable relations existing between things, relations between signs and words and the represented objects, laws of sympathy in general.[30]

The composite idea of magical milieu-force is similar to that of *mana*, which is the basis of this necessary idea of a sphere superimposed on reality, animated by spirits into which the magician penetrates, and where the rites take place. In addition, the *mana* legitimises the magician's power and the transfers of properties and influences. An expression of "collective forces", it functions after the fashion of an *unconscious category of collective thinking* which conditions, governs and forms the magical representations. Its role is justly expressed by the facts. Thus, it only exists in the consciousness of individuals precisely because of its existence in society and is therefore variable with its own evolution in accordance with the diverse societies. In my opinion, the *mana* could partly correspond to the collective imaginary or Durkheim's idealism, "creator of reality".

This system of magic is a system of social values in the same way that language is a system of signs and therefore of relative values.

> [T]he magical value of persons or things results from the relative position they occupy within society or in relation to society. The two separate notions of magical virtue and social position coincide in so far as one depends on the other. Basically in magic it is always a matter of the respective values recognized by society. These values do not depend, in fact, on the intrinsic qualities of a thing or a person, but on the status or rank attributed to them by all-powerful public opinion, by its prejudices. They are social facts not experimental facts.[31]

70 Symbols, symbolism and symbolisation

Mauss explains that the idea of *mana* is the very idea of these values.

> Here we come face to face with the whole idea on which magic is founded, in fact with magic itself. It goes without saying that ideas like this have no raison d'être outside society, that they are absurd as far as pure reason is concerned and that they derive purely and simply from the functioning of collective life.[32]

As an unconscious category of collective thought, the *mana* is the basis of the "value judgments" constitutive of magic and religion, which are always the object of social consent expressing a social need, but also of a unanimous belief in the truth of certain ideas, in the effectiveness of certain gestures. Finally, prior to the magical experiments done to confirm those ideas, the value judgments are the object of a collective affirmation. In addition, the *mana* attributes diverse qualities to the diverse objects entering into its system, chosen arbitrarily for the most part. Moreover, it imposes the sorting of things, separates certain ones and unites the others.

Magic is closely allied with the whole system of collective prohibitions, including religious prohibitions. It has a veritable predilection for forbidden things and uses the violations of taboos to its own advantage.

While it is essentially the expression of collective desires and needs, generators of illusion, "[t]hanks to the idea of mana, magic – the domain of wish-fulfilment – is shown to have plenty of rationalism".[33]

Finally, Mauss and Hubert concluded with a reflection which would be taken up again in 1924 in the form of *the symbolic activity of the mind* and of the primary form of human thought, *symbolic thought*:

> "We are confident that ... we shall find magical origins in those forms of collective representations which have since become the basis for individual understanding".[34]

"Real and Practical Relations between Psychology and Sociology"[35]

Among the recent services psychology had rendered to sociology over the past twenty years, Mauss listed some notions formulated by psychologists which stem from the study of the consciousness in its relationship with the body: those of vigour and of feeblemindedness, psychosis, symbol and instinct. It is quite evidently the notion of symbol which will primarily be of interest here, then that of instinct because, as Mauss explained in this paper the notion of symbol is entirely ours, having originated in religion and law. He said there that he and Durkheim had long been teaching that one can only be in communion and communicate among human beings through symbols, through permanent, common signs external to individual mental states, which are just simply successive, through signs of groups of states later taken for realities. They had long thought, Mauss continued, that one of the characteristics of social facts is precisely its symbolic aspect. In most collective representations, it is not a matter of a single representation of a single thing, but of a representation chosen arbitrarily, or more or less arbitrarily, to signify others and to require practices. They had become sure of their theory by the very fact of their agreement with psychologists. If what they had been told is true of the individual consciousness, it is all the more so of the collective consciousness.

After having presented symbols as instruments of social communication, and looking at the symbolic aspect of social facts, Mauss looked into the symbolic activity of the mind, collective as well as individual. He considered the activity of the collective mind to be even more symbolic than that of the individual mind, but to be so in exactly the same sense. He explained that from this point of view there was only a difference of intensity, of kind. There is no difference of type. This idea of symbol could be used concurrently with preceding ones and, put all together, could explain important elements of myths, rites, beliefs and faith in terms of their effectiveness, of illusion, religious hallucination, aesthetics, lying and collective delirium and its rectification.

As for the *notion of instinct*, he cited Babinski, Monakow and Rivers, who had taught him about the considerable place accorded to this part of mental life in the interpretation of hysterias.

Mauss explained that, for psychologists, the idea, the representation and the act, be it a matter of fleeing or capturing, do not only translate some function or state of mind as it relates to things, but also manifest at the same time, always in a partial, symbolic manner, the relationship existing between things and the body and above all the instinct, "*Treib*", of every being, of its psychophysiological mechanisms all set up. But if such is the instinct's share when it comes to individual psychology, it is even greater when it comes to collective psychology. For what is common to human beings is not only the identical images which produce the same things in their consciousness, but also, above all, the identity of the instincts affected by these things. He had said that human beings communicate through symbols, but more precisely they can only have these symbols and communicate by means of them because they have the same instincts. The exaltations, the ecstasies that create symbols are proliferations of the instinct, something which his friend Rivers had demonstrated well.

What can sociology do for psychology?

Mauss considered that the facts of collective consciousness represent one of the principal inventories of observable facts of consciousness. Their repetition, their statistical nature and the fact that they are common to many individuals are characteristic and make them "typical documents" about human behaviour. This is why he affirmed that sociologists possess the most extensive record of psychological facts, both normal and pathological, and of cases of symbolism, unlike psychologists, who can only lay hold of them fairly rarely and often in pathological situations. Among the examples, he cited in particular "thanatomania" – the

72 Symbols, symbolism and symbolisation

violent negation of the instinct to live by the social instinct – normal in Australians and Maoris and the "amok" or hallucinatory rage of vendetta in the Maoris, very many Malayans and Polynesians.

Mauss then continues saying that the cries and the words, the gestures and the rites, for example, are signs and symbols of etiquette and morals, which are basically translations. They in fact first translate the presence of the group, but they also additionally express the actions and reactions of the instincts of its members, the direct needs of each and of all, of their personality, of their reciprocal relations. What, he asks, are the words, the greetings, the presents solemnly exchanged and received, and necessarily reciprocated on pain of war, if not symbols? And what, if not symbols, are beliefs which lead to faith, which inspire, and the intermingling of certain things and the prohibitions which separate the things from one another?

Here, Mauss was therefore stressing the existence of a twofold relationship of *translation* and *expression* among social facts and states, collective needs and social relationships, as well as the role played by instincts in the members.

It is then that in all these domains of social life the general psychological fact appears completely clearly, because it is precisely social, that is to say common to all the participants, therefore stripped of individual variants. He then explains that there is in social facts a sort of natural laboratory experiment making the harmonics go away, leaving only, so to speak, the pure sound. Mauss came to write of the "phenomena of totality" to which sociology, which refers to study of the "complete human being", is inevitably exposed. He considered that in reality, in the science of sociology, one hardly or even almost never finds human beings divided into faculties, except when it comes to pure literature or pure science. One is always dealing with their completely whole bodies and minds given at the same time and all at once. Body, soul and society are all fundamentally mixed together there. One is no longer interested in special facts about one or another part of the mind, but in facts of a very complex kind, the most complex imaginable. It is what he presumed to call phenomena of totality, in which not only the group takes part, but also through it, all the personalities, all the individuals in their mental, social, moral and, above all, bodily or material entirety.

The Gift: The Form and Reason for Exchange in Archaic Societies

On the basis of an exploration of social facts concerning the laws and economies of some Oceanian (Melanesian and Polynesian) and northwestern American societies, Mauss proposed to identify some stages which had led to the institutions and fundamental principles behind the laws and economies of our western societies.

The "archaic" form of exchange, that of "gifts presented and reciprocated" or "principle of exchange-gift", had to be that of societies which had gone beyond the phase of the system of "total services", but which nevertheless had not reached that of the purely individual contract, of the market, of actual selling

Symbols, symbolism and symbolisation **73**

and the notion of price reckoned in coinage. However, we live in societies that, since first the Semitic and then Greek and Roman civilisations, have invented the distinctions between real law and personal law, between persons and things; have separated selling from gift and exchange where persons and things merge; have isolated moral obligation and contract; and above all have conceived of the difference existing between rites, laws and interests. Thus, through a veritable revolution, they went beyond this economy of gift, which was too expensive and sumptuous, incompatible with the development of the market, commerce and production, and essentially anti-economic.

On the other hand, in the economic and legal systems preceding ours, it was collectivities (clans, tribes, families), not individuals, which made obligations to one another, exchanged and entered into contracts. They met, confronted and opposed one another, according to Mauss, either in groups meeting face to face on the spot, or through their chiefs, or in both ways at once. Moreover, what they exchanged were not exclusively economically useful goods and wealth, but above all

> acts of politeness, banquets, rituals, military services, women, children, dances, festivals, fairs in which economic transaction is only one element, and in which the passing on of wealth is only one feature of a much more general and enduring contract.[36]

This "system of total services", as Mauss called it, constituted "the most ancient system of economy and law that we can find or of which we can conceive. It forms the base from which the morality of the exchange-through-gift has flowed".[37] It calls to mind, notably, the *potlatch* or system of exchanges–gifts of an agonistic type in North American societies and the *kula*, a sort of "grand potlatch" described by Malinowski.

According to Mauss, moral and material life and exchange function in these societies in a form that is both disinterested and obligatory. The circulation of things is identified with that of rights and persons. In addition, *this obligation is expressed in a collective and symbolic fashion.* It assumes an aspect centring on the interest attached to the things exchanged, which are never completely detached from those engaging in the exchange. The communion and alliance they establish are relatively indissoluble. Mauss considered that this *symbol of social life* "serves merely to reflect somewhat directly the manner in which the subgroups in these segmented societies, archaic in type and constantly enmeshed with one another, feel that they are everything to one another".[38]

This system of exchanges–gifts involves three obligations: that of giving, that of receiving and that of reciprocating. But, Mauss points out, if

> one gives things and returns them, it is because one is giving and returning "respects" – we will say "courtesies". Yet it is also because by giving one is giving *oneself* and if one gives *oneself*, it is because one "owes" *oneself* – one's person and one's goods – to others.[39]

74 Symbols, symbolism and symbolisation

Mauss discusses the difference in the notion of self-interest in these societies, notably potlatch societies, and ours. In the former, people act in their own self-interest, but in a different way. They hoard, but do so in order to spend, to place under obligation. Furthermore, they exchange, but it is above all an exchange of luxury items, ornaments, clothes or things consumed immediately, such as banquets. While the notion of individual self-interest and pursuit of utility is recent, the Latin word *interest* was originally an accounting technique. According to Mauss, the "victory of rationalism and mercantilism was needed before the notions of profit and the individual, raised to the level of principles, were introduced".[40]

Finally, Mauss maintained that it is our western civilisation that has recently transformed human beings into "economic animals", into *homo oeconomicus*, without however eliminating purely irrational expenditure, which is still a common practice, as among members of the nobility.

Commentaries, remarks and reflections

Let us explore the evolution of Mauss' ideas from *A General Theory of Magic* up to *The Gift*.

As early as *A General Theory of Magic* (1902–1903), Mauss and Hubert advanced a conception of symbols and symbolism breaking with the Durkheimian conception. Karsenti (1997) in fact considered that their attempt to conceptualise magical phenomena as social phenomena on the basis of a linguistic model enabled them to isolate the problems of symbolism systematically for the first time and led them to an initial "symbolic formalisation of the social" unprecedented up until then in French socio-anthropological thought. In that respect, Karsenti considers that it was a matter of an "inaugural act". It is worth pointing out that as a philologist, in particular, Mauss had already directly or indirectly confronted problems of language, translation and interpretation.

Symbol, symbolism and symbolisation in Mauss

Thus, from the time of *A General Theory of Magic*, symbols appeared empty of all representative content, and Mauss emphasised their *formal constitution* within the framework of a system of signs and social values represented by magic.[41] From then on, symbols no longer connected predetermined terms but signs, which were themselves relative entities. From this completely new perspective, symbolism would designate the dynamic activity through which signs are determined and produce their meaning through the sole play of their mutual relations. However, while Mauss refused to distinguish between sign and symbol, he did not reduce either symbols to linguistic signs or language to the Saussurian conception, of which he had little knowledge.

Moreover, the adoption of the point of view of magic causes a shift from the dimension of *objectification* to that of *signification* within the symbol itself,

Symbols, symbolism and symbolisation **75**

something which calls into question the Durkheimian subordination of symbols to representations. Indeed, according to Mauss, it is not because the symbol represents the social that it constitutes a signifying entity for individual consciousnesses. Rather, it is this function of signification itself that asserts itself as preeminent and as a primordial condition of the social. Thus freed from the concept of representation, symbolism assumes an autonomous, founding nature it could not have had in Durkheim's eyes.

From another perspective, Maussian symbols form "chains" and only exist in networks that constitute symbolisms: those of a rite, a religion, a culture. In addition, these symbolisms have their own order. Indeed, this world of signs and symbols, which has its own specific nature, its own reality and its own order, cannot be fused with the world of experience. Anthropologically speaking, this set of symbolisms can be designated by the *symbolic*.

As for *mana*, defined by Mauss as an unconscious category of collective thought, it draws its capacity to make things and beings signifiers of the one unconscious formal system of relations that it implements on its own level. Its function is actually to realize the unconscious operations of symbolisation. According to Lévi-Strauss, it is

> the conscious expression of a *semantic function*, whose role is to enable symbolic thinking to operate despite the contradiction inherent in it. … a simple form, or to be more accurate, a symbol in its pure state, therefore liable to take on any symbolic content whatever.[42]

Naturally, but if it is a matter of a symbolic language or system of signs and social values, Mauss explained, the latter are only the symbolic expression of needs and collective desires. Apart from its rationality, magic is the "domain of desire", he wrote.

What about "Real and Practical Relations between Psychology and Sociology" (1924)?

In Karsenti's opinion, it is hard to keep from reading the passages devoted to symbolism in the lecture given to the Société française de psychologie in 1924 as a late echo of the call of 1903.[43] While Tarot considers this lecture as marking the birth of the anthropology of the symbolic, or the shift from Durkheimian sociology toward the problems of the symbolic,[44] Mauss realised that it was necessary to replace the study of problems surrounding representation and mental states, which had dominated philosophy and psychology, with the study of problems surrounding signs. Introducing the study of problems about signs and symbols offers a way out of the cumbersome collective consciousness.

Mauss presented symbols there as being common, "permanent" signs "external to individual mental states" that enable people to communicate with one another but also to be in communion. These characteristics attest in this way to

76 Symbols, symbolism and symbolisation

their non-individual, social origin. The very notion of symbol is the mediating agency discovered by Mauss to connect psychology and sociology, the psychological to the social and the individual to the collective.

Indeed, as Tarot emphasised in *Le symbolique et le sacré*, the progress made by psychology between the 1890s and the 1920s brought to the fore this notion, which had shaped Mauss' work from within for over twenty years. It therefore completely naturally mediated between these two disciplines for Mauss. From then on, the psychic and the social become two modalities and two points of view about the same human reality of the total human being and the total social fact.

From this completely new perspective, symbolisation was going to play out and be replayed on the interface of all these dimensions. It is therefore not the exclusive property of sociologists but also concerns psychologists, even biologists as well.

Mauss also made several suggestions regarding the "symbolic aspect" of the social fact and about the world of teeming symbolic relationships that all social life constitutes. Then, he brought up the fundamental, central notion of the *symbolic activity of the mind*, both collective and individual, of unconscious nature, the former proving more symbolic than the latter. According to him, it is only a matter there of a difference of intensity and species, but not of kind, something which makes it possible to explain important elements of, for example, myths, rites, beliefs and collective delirium. Nevertheless, this notion of the symbolic activity of the mind also functions as a mediation-connection between the collective and individual fields. *Thus, there is no longer any split between the social and the individual, but rather transitions, mediations and relationships of interdependence.* Mauss, by the way, entertained the hypothesis of intermediaries establishing an unbroken thread running from the collective psychical structure to individual psychical structure.

In addition, he fully recognized that *symbolic thought is the first form of human thought*, underlying all thought, and he strove to identify its activity in all the strata of the social. The very condition of exercising symbolic thought rests, according to Lévi-Strauss in *Introduction to the Work of Marcel Mauss*, on this relationship of complementarity between signifier and signified.

Moreover, Mauss did not hesitate to set up relationships of translation between all the levels of the real, between the sociological and the psychological, between society and individuals, but also at the very heart of the sociological, between the economic, the social, the political, the religious, the aesthetic and finally between the psychological, the sociological and the biological.

As Tarot has observed, everything social is symbolic. Meaning and force circulate among all the levels of its reality, and these levels are translated one into the other. Everything acts on everything.

Mauss identified the mechanism of production of meaning that is at the heart of social life and that is, in a sense, prior to it, even if it is only actualized, realized in and by it. Adopting the expression of his colleague, the English neuropsychologist Head, he used the term *symbolic function* to designate this mechanism.

Finally, Mauss' thought enables one to go beyond Durkheim's finding that social life would not be possible without symbolism, the role of which is also to represent it to individual consciousnesses: it affirms that *symbolism is what makes social life possible and produces it*. Symbolism is just simply a necessary condition of any group. It is the condition of the existence of groups as groups. The *symbolic* is therefore an order of things unto itself and functionally necessary to the human world.[45]

Moreover, Mauss came to think that social particularities specifically result from processes of symbolisation, that is to say, from agreements that are non-universal, therefore *arbitrary*, but are particular and necessary, or at least functional, for people obliged to live in groups. He wrote in "Civilizational Forms" (1929),

> *all social phenomenon* have one essential attribute: be it a symbol, a word, an instrument, or an institution ... even if this distinguishing characteristic is the most rational thing possible, and the most human, it is still fundamentally *arbitrary* in nature.
>
> All social phenomena are to some degree the work of the collective will. To speak of human will is to imply choice among different possible options ... everything has a type and a manner. In addition to its intrinsic nature and form, in many cases it also has a distinctive mode of utilization. The realm of the social is the realm of modalities.[46]

Thus, each society produces its own symbolisations. Mauss then clearly set down the terms of the dialectic of the human universal and the social particular.

On the subject of instincts, another notion Mauss discussed and developed, what interested him about them was the relationship obtaining between representations, acts, the body and especially instincts and things. In addition, he considered that this part of instinct was even much greater when it came to collective psychology. He in fact believed that people can only produce and communicate through symbols because they share the same instincts, of which states of exaltation, effervescence, "ecstasies", creators of ideals and symbols are "proliferations".

This is something which has not been sufficiently noted by Karsenti and Tarot, not to mention Lévi-Strauss and his exclusion of the body. Indeed, just as in Durkheim, idealism and symbolism form a functional and therefore necessary pair, in Mauss we could associate instincts and symbols.

Mauss' essay on *The Gift*

What does this study tell us about Maussian symbolism?

Just as magic is, the gift is an exemplary illustration of his conceptual elaboration in the field of social life itself, understood as a living system of exchanges.

Tarot believes that *The Gift* impressed upon people the idea that *gifts are a form of symbolism*. Whatever forms they take, gifts witness fundamental forms of the social relationship coming into being. They bring together *groups* or *legal*

78 Symbols, symbolism and symbolisation

entities through concrete people who give. Mauss saw well that gifts are symbolic because they signify and act first of all on social ties to create or recreate. Human beings are condemned to speak with one another and establish bonds. Gifts are not only symbolic of the social bond but also bring about the bond and objectivize the otherwise invisible reality.

Plunging into depths less temporal than structural, Karsenti has suggested that gifts bring to light what might be supposed to be an "originary form" of the social bond. He has said that what Mauss was unveiling is one of those human rocks upon which our societies are built, one of those fundamental reasons behind human activity. Gift are precisely realities of this type.[47]

While Durkheim proposed a sociological theory of symbolisation, Mauss introduced a symbolic theory of society fitting into the framework of an elaboration of an anthropology of the symbolic, as Tarot thinks, as a deep orientation that he made sociology and anthropology adopt from then on but also as a project to which he invited specialists in the human and social sciences.

Freud, symbolism and symbolisation

Symbolism and symbolisation inaugurated psychoanalysis on the basis of psychoneurotic symptoms and their "symbolic" meaning, primarily hysterical conversion. By uncovering the relationships between manifest symptoms and their latent meanings reflecting repressed unconscious contents, Freud uncovered, and at the same time explored, the processes of individual symbolisation relating to an essential psychic function.

It was only during a second phase that dream symbolism or the *symbolic* entered into the history of psychoanalysis and the young psychoanalytical movement. Then Freud discovered other forms of symbolisation, such as circumcision, a collective ritual practice he began reflecting upon in *Totem and Taboo* (1912–1913) and, later on, children's games, as another form of individual symbolisation, which is described in *Beyond the Pleasure Principle* (1920).

Freud grew aware of the symbolising and symbolic dimension of the analytic arrangement he had set up owing to its mode of functioning based on a three-term structure (that of patient, analyst and the third agency of the setting, including money) conditioning the unfolding of the process of symbolisation in patients, notably through verbalisation.

He also realized that transference actualises another form of displacement of a representation to another having symbolic and symptomatic value and underscores in exemplary fashion the role and significance of the lost object in the appearing of a process of symbolisation.

So, I shall take a look at four forms of symbolic production:

Symptoms: primarily hysterical conversion; then little Hans' phobia; the symbolism or symbolic of dreams; the bobbin game; and, finally, circumcision as a form of collective symbolisation within the framework of ritual practices.

Unlike the way I chose to present Durkheim's and Mauss' ideas, I shall successively present each topic, including texts, followed by remarks, commentaries and reflections supported by the ideas of other authors, such as Jean Laplanche and Alain Gibeault.

Symptoms: discovery of a process of individual symbolisation correlative to the creation of psychoanalysis

The object of the first text on defence psychoneuroses (1894) is the fact that neuroses have *meaning*. Symptoms are symbolic substitutes for a repressed content, developing by way of what Freud called "false connections". The work of analysis then consists of taking symptoms back to their true *meaning* by re-establishing the "false connection" and recovering the original representation.

In several passages of his *Studies on Hysteria* (1895),[48] Freud distinguishes between a twofold determinism, *associative* and *symbolic*, of symptoms of conversion. However, this determinism, called symbolic determinism, is not strictly individual. It includes a collective portion borrowed from culture, common and shared, within which language plays a major mediating role in the operation of conversion. This is why, when Freud writes of symbolisation in these texts, one must avoid any risk of confusion and understand it as a process which is both individual and collective in nature, unlike what is called associative determinism, which produces "mnesic symbols" of traumatic experiences and is therefore strictly individual in nature.

By way of illustration, let us look at the exemplary case history of Fräulein Elisabeth von R... who had suffered from pains in her legs for more than two years and from astasia-abasia when Freud met her for the first time during the fall of 1892. In this account we find the principal mentions of "mnesic symbol" and "symbolisation", but also this distinction between associative connection and symbolisation. Freud wrote,

> We might perhaps suppose that the patient had formed an association between her painful mental impressions and the bodily pains which she happened to be experiencing at the same time, and that now, in her life of memories, she was using her physical feelings as a symbol of her mental ones. But it remained unexplained what her motives might have been for making a substitution of this kind and at what moment it had taken place. These, incidentally, were not the kind of questions that physicians were in the habit of raising. We were usually content with the statement that the patient was constitutionally a hysteric, liable to develop hysterical symptoms under the pressure of intense excitations *of whatever kind*.[49]

Here, Freud mentions the existence of a *relationship of association* between mental impressions and bodily pain felt at the same time, then *the psychic inscription of this association in the form of mnesic trace* determining the later operation of *substitution* of the bodily sensation for the psychic pain, thus becoming its *mnesic symbol*.

80 Symbols, symbolism and symbolisation

This mechanism of substitution would be called *conversion*, which procures for the patient the benefit of being spared an unbearable psychic state at the cost of a *split consciousness*, correlative to the separation between the group of intolerable representations and the bodily suffering.

However, Freud introduced us to a notion of *afterwardness* by explaining that these bodily pains, products of conversion and mnesic symbols, only appeared in a second period, in the *memories of impressions* of the first period, which then became *traumatic* in nature, hence the finding that "conversion can result equally from fresh symptoms and from recollected ones. This hypothesis completely explains the apparent contradiction that we observed between the events of Fräulein Elisabeth v. R.'s illness and her analysis".[50]

As for symbolisation, it is a matter of a second mechanism contributing to the patient's astasia, which did not seem predominant but which, according to Freud, particularly reinforced it. Thus, the sick person had created or aggravated the functional trouble, built on suffering, by means of *symbolisation*. She had in fact

> found in the astasia-abasia a somatic expression for her lack of an independent position and her inability to make any alteration in her circumstances, and that such phrases as "not being able to take a single step forward", "not having anything to lean upon", served as a bridge for this new act of conversion.[51]

Consequently, Freud conceived of this astasia-abasia as being a matter of a "functional paralysis based on psychical associations but also one based on symbolization".[52]

He furthermore gives most beautiful examples of symbolisation encountered in another patient, Frau Cäcilie, who suffered, among other things, from an extremely violent facial neuralgia which, as in Elisabeth, was a matter of a twofold mechanism, but also of symptoms through *simple symbolisation*:

> When a girl of fifteen, she was lying in bed, under the watchful eye of her strict grandmother. The girl suddenly gave a cry, she had felt a penetrating pain in her forehead between her eyes, which lasted for weeks. During the analysis of this pain, which was reproduced after nearly thirty years, she told me that her grandmother had given her a look so "piercing" that it had gone right into her brain. (She had been afraid that the old woman was viewing her with suspicion.) As she told me this thought she broke into a loud laugh, and the pain once more disappeared. In this instance I can detect nothing other than the mechanism of symbolization, which has its place, in some sense, midway between autosuggestion and conversion.[53]

He considered that this *conversion by symbolisation* "seems to call for the presence of a higher degree of hysterical modification", unlike conversion "on the basis of simultaneity, where there is also an associative link".[54]

Symbols, symbolism and symbolisation **81**

In addition, Freud engaged in particularly fruitful reflections on the sociocultural part of the determination of hysterical symbolisation mediated by language, a shared legacy and collective possession, unlike associative determinism, which is individual in nature. He expressed himself thus:

> It is my opinion, however, that when a hysteric creates a somatic expression for an emotionally-coloured idea by symbolization, this depends less than one would imagine on personal or voluntary factors. In taking the verbal expression literally and in feeling the "stab in the heart" or the "slap in the face" after some slighting remark as a real event, the hysteric is not taking liberties with words, but is simply reviving once more the sensations to which the verbal expression owes its justification. How has it come about that we speak of someone who has been slighted as being "stabbed to the heart" unless the slight had in fact been accompanied by a precordial sensation which could suitably be described in that phrase and unless it was identifiable by that sensation? What could be more probable than that figure of speech "swallowing something", which we use in talking of an insult to which no rejoinder has been made, did in fact originate from the innervatory sensations which arrive in the pharynx when we refrain from speaking and prevent ourselves from reacting to the insult? All these sensations and innervations belong to the field of "The Expression of the Emotions", which, as Darwin [1872] has taught us, consists of actions which originally had a meaning and served a purpose. These may now for the most part have become so much weakened that the expression of them in words seems to us only to be a figurative picture of them, whereas in all probability the description was once meant literally; and hysteria is right in restoring the original meaning of the words in depicting its unusually strong innervations. Indeed, it is perhaps wrong to say that hysteria creates these sensations by symbolization. It may be that it does not take the linguistic usage as its model at all, but that both hysteria and linguistic usage alike draw their material from a common source.[55]

However, he explained that this symbolisation of psychic states in bodily states mediated by the use of a common language essentially concerns pains and neuralgias, which excludes other symptoms such as epileptiform convulsions, hemianaesthesia and contraction of the field of vision.

Finally, in the case history of Dora, he stated several propositions, adding complexity to the elaboration of psychoneurotic symptoms and over-determining their meaning:

> According to a rule which I had found confirmed over and over again by experience, though I had not yet ventured to erect it into a general principle, a symptom signifies the representation – the realization – of a phantasy with a sexual content, that is to say, it signifies a sexual situation. It would be

82 Symbols, symbolism and symbolisation

better to say that at least *one* of the meanings of a symptom is the representation of a sexual phantasy, but that no such limitation is imposed upon the content of its other meanings. Anyone who takes up psycho-analytic work will quickly discover that a symptom has more than one meaning and serves to represent several unconscious mental processes simultaneously. And I should like to add that in my estimation a single unconscious mental process or phantasy will scarcely ever suffice for the production of a symptom.

An opportunity very soon occurred for interpreting Dora's nervous cough in this way by means of an imagined sexual situation.[56]

Ultimately, hysterical symptoms were from the beginning considered and designated by Freud as symbols, "mnesic symbols", of a memory, or a repressed phantasy, of a traumatic nature, that is to say as something definitively inscribed in the body, that of the hysterical person. Resulting from a process of substitution of a bodily state for a psychic state, from a conversion linked to an associative connection, it was therefore a matter of an individual symbolisation, not designated as such, that linked symptoms, conscious symbols, to things symbolized unconsciously. In this way, according to Alain Gibeault in *Les chemins de la symbolisation* (2010),[57] Freud introduced a new dimension into this discovery of symbolisation. It is a matter of an intrapsychic–individual dimension.

In so doing, the hysteria of conversion showed him the path to follow to highlight the body's symbolising function and its essential link to the memory. Points of reference were then established with respect to the significance of the body and instincts as "sources" of symbolisation and language. More precisely, this process of symbolisation at work in hysterical conversion is to be conceived of as an activity connecting the affects, which finds its limits, its source and its *raison d'être* in the body. However, Gibeault has pointed out that hysteria of conversion would rather be a matter of failure in this work of representation and linking of affects. This is how these specific features of the hysteria of conversion, like those of the other psychoneurotic symptoms – obsessional and phobic – provided Freud with an opening onto the universality of the symbolic function.

Let us now examine, on the basis of Freud's *Papers on Metapsychology* (1915),[58] the phobia of little Hans, the development of which involves four phases.

According to Freud, the *first phase* is that of the repression of an anxiogenic instinctual motion, the love of the father, which will be directed toward the representation–representative, while the quantum of affect will be partially repressed. The *second phase* concerns the attempt of the repressed to return, during which the affect of love – then liberated from its paternal representation which is forbidden access to the consciousness – succeeds in passing censorship in a free form, transformed into anxiety, something which generates the crisis of anxiety. The *third phase* is characterised by the anchoring–connecting of this affect of paroxysmal anxiety onto a substitutive representation, the horse, becoming an anxiogenic animal, whose function is multiple: first of all, it is a matter of a symbol-substitute for the father, whom it represents and masks at the same time, just as it keeps him from returning to consciousness by constituting a counter-investment. In addition, this representation anchors the anguish by rationalising it. Indeed, Hans can justify his fear of horses in various different respects. This representation thus makes it possible to localise the danger, both in psychic space and in the space of external reality. And in the latter space it is the object of a secondary combat. The *fourth phase* constitutes this secondary combat around the phobic object, which is then an instinctual offshoot. It is definitely a matter of a projection onto the reality of the instinctual danger. The neurosis ultimately substitutes an external danger, much easier to avoid and to control, for a danger of internal origin, the love of the father at the cost of sacrifices and a loss of freedom.

Having reached the end of our exploration of these two types of psychoneurotic symptoms, what did Freud ultimately discover?

On the one hand, he discovered that individual symbolisation associates two representations, that it in fact substitutes one representation for another and is therefore a mode of "indirect representation". On the other hand, he discovered that it also connects an affect and a representation, the affect indissociably being that of desire and anxiety. He likewise understood that symbolisation is above all the result of a process presupposing both the ability to *represent* an absent *object* and a subject capable of *knowing* that the symbol is not the object symbolised.

Of course, but in different sense, "symbolising conversion" draws from a common cultural source through the mediation of language, hence another form of symbolisation, less individual and more collective, which will meet up with the symbolic of dreams.

In a certain way, little Hans' phobia proves to be particularly exemplary in the sense that, like any symptom, it in fact displays the twofold dimension and the twofold meaning of individual symbolisation: symbolisation of a representation and therefore of a repressed representative content (the father complex), but also symbolisation in the sense of connecting the affect, in this case, the affect of anxiety.

The symbolism of dreams or the symbolic

In his *Introductory Lectures on Psycho-Analysis* (1915–1916), Freud declared that dream symbolism had not been discovered by psychoanalysis. Rather, he attributed its discovery to the philosopher Karl Albert Scherner, whose discoveries, Freud maintained, psychoanalysis had confirmed while modifying them in a truly decisive way.[59]

The years 1909–1915 represented a historical period of flowering of the notion of symbolism for the young psychoanalytical movement. Besides Stekel's book, *Sex and Dreams: The Language of Dreams* (1911),[60] other colleagues, for example Carl Jung, Otto Rank, Hanns Sachs and then Ernest Jones, become interested in it and published works on the subject.

84 Symbols, symbolism and symbolisation

While the task of *The Interpretation of Dreams* (1900) is defined in opposition to the theories and practices of the so-called key to dreams of Antiquity, it was through the writings of his disciples on the symbolic that Freud had to go back on both his initial estimation of those practices and on his own technique of association to admit that, in certain cases, when it was a matter of a particularly obvious, widespread symbol, one could directly accede to the interpretation.

Thus, in his "Preface to the Third Edition" of *The Interpretation of Dreams*, dated 1911, he said that when he had written it in 1899,

> [i]t was my hope that dream-interpretation would help to make possible the psychological analysis of neuroses; since then a deeper comprehension of neuroses has reacted in turn upon our view of dreams. The theory of dream-interpretation has itself developed further in a direction on which insufficient stress had been laid in the first edition of this book. My own experience, as well as the works of Wilhelm Stekel and others, have since taught me to form a truer estimate of the extent and importance of symbolism in dreams (or rather in unconscious thinking).[61]

However, by 1900, several factors had already charted the course this theory of symbolism would take and, among them, what Freud called "typical dreams". This notion would be developed considerably in the 1911 edition, once the theory of symbolism had been formulated, which in and of itself affirms the universality of certain unconscious contents.

What would come to be added, Jean Laplanche has declared, is the affirmation of a genuine *antagonism* between what we can call individual symbolisation and the typical symbolic:

- antagonism in the mode in which they arise – where the latter is significant, the former is "mute";
- in the methods of investigation – free association or key to dreams;
- in the content finally – which refers, depending on the cases, to individual "sources" or to origins common to all people.[62]

Freud defined *symbolic relationships* – notably in his *Introductory Lectures on Psycho-Analysis* (1915–1916) – as "constant translations for a number of dream-elements"; this element itself has been described as a "'symbol' of the unconscious dream-thought".[63] This relationship between symbols and what is symbolised was a one-to-one relationship based on "resemblance", analogy or evolving towards the natural analogy (of form, size, function, frequency, etc.). However, unlike Stekel, Freud considered that the imagination does not admit to just anything, and a long, stiff object cannot be a female symbol because of its very form, which imposes limits on the imagination.[64] The essence of this type of relationship is therefore a relationship of comparisons of a particular kind among diverse

Symbols, symbolism and symbolisation **85**

objects, which leads to one's being constantly put in the place of the other, something which results from their concordance in diverse persons.

Freud considered that with

> a number of symbols, the comparison which underlies them is obvious. But again there are other symbols in regard to which we must ask ourselves where we are to look for the common element, the *tertium comparationis* of this supposed comparison.[65]

A number of symbols common elsewhere do not, or quite rarely, appear in dreams, and those of dreams are absent in the other domains, or are very small in number. According to Freud, the field of the *symbolic*, or system of fixed symbols, was in fact extraordinarily large, that of dreams representing but a small part. In addition, in those other domains, the symbolic was quite obviously not only sexual, unlike in dreams where the immense majority of symbols were almost exclusively used to represent the sphere of sexual life (genitals, sexed processes, sexual relations). However, other symbols would represent the human body as a whole, the human person, parents, children, brothers and sisters, birth, nudity and death.

Consequently, Freud observed a distinct contrast between the wealth of sexual symbols and the paucity of things symbolised by multiple, quasi equivalent symbols, and therefore a multivocity of symbols and a sameness of interpretations. In addition, he could not refrain from assuming the existence of a particularly close relationship between genuine symbols and what is sexual. However, while the relationship binding symbols to what is symbolised is woven out of multiple connections, strictly individual connections prove, for Freud, to be of primordial importance.

Besides, he considered that in dreamwork there is not any symbolising activity specific to the psyche, but that dreams use symbolisations which are present, "lie ready to hand and are complete once and for all"[66] in unconscious thought because they better satisfy the requirements of the distortion–formation of dreams. Indeed, "symbolism is a second and independent factor in the distortion of dreams", of which censorship readily makes use since it also leads to the "strangeness and incomprehensibility of dreams".[67]

Lying "ready to hand" and being "complete once and for all" means being available right from the very beginning of the life of every dreamer, something which raises questions of both a phylogenetic and an ontogenetic nature: How did humanity create symbols? How do individuals inherit and appropriate them?

The ultimate meaning of this symbolic relation seemed to him to be

> of a genetic character. Things that are symbolically connected today were probably united in prehistoric times by conceptual and linguistic identity. The symbolic relation seems to be a relic and a mark of former identity. ... A number of symbols are as old as language itself, while others

86 Symbols, symbolism and symbolisation

(e.g. "airship", "Zeppelin") are being coined continuously down to the present time. [1914.][68]

It was therefore a matter of "an ancient but extinct mode of expression, of which different pieces have survived in different fields, one piece only here, another only there, a third, perhaps, in slightly modified forms in several fields", something which for Freud was suggestive of "a 'basic language' of which all these symbolic relations would be 'residues'", adopting thus an expression of his patient, Senatspräsident Schreber.[69]

Consequently, with the theory of *the* symbolic, there reappears the possibility of a certain universal language which would allow an *a priori* deciphering, a trans-individual deciphering in certain cases or on certain points. One has the impression that, beyond the diversity of cultures and of languages, the subjects have this "basic language" at their disposal.

But then, Freud inquired into the source of our knowledge of the meaning of symbols and symbolic relations of dreams about which dreamers do not give us, or give us so little, information. He wrote

> that we learn it from very different sources – from fairy tales and myths, from buffoonery and jokes, from folklore (that is, from knowledge about popular manners and customs, sayings and songs) and from poetic and colloquial linguistic usage. In all these directions we come upon the same symbolism, and in some of them we can understand it without further instruction. If we go into these sources in detail, we shall find so many parallels to dream-symbolism that we cannot fail to be convinced of our interpretations.[70]

Indeed, this *symbolism* – which is not peculiar to dreams and, furthermore, is shared with psychoneuroses – is in fact "characteristic of unconscious ideation among the people".[71] It is therefore not only individual, but also collective in nature. We find there what he was already formulating about the sources common to the symbolism of hysterical conversion.

However, in *Moses and Monotheism* (1939), Freud reminded us that "what may be operative in an individual's psychical life may include not only what he has experienced himself but also things that were innately present in him at his birth", such as thinking and instinctual dispositions, "elements with a phylogenetic origin – an *archaic heritage*". He mentioned "in the first place, the universality of symbolism in language", an "original knowledge" detectable in children and in the dreams of adults, dating back from the time when language developed and suggesting the existence of "the inheritance of an intellectual disposition similar to the ordinary inheritance of an instinctual disposition"[72] actualising during the historical development of speech.

The symbolic relation never learned by the individual should therefore be considered a phylogenetic inheritance.

Thus dreams, but also neuroses, would be "repositories" of contents of the *archaic inheritance*, just as are the cultural products, such as the most ancient legends and ancient customs, among others. Moreover, Freud explained that it was in the realm of psychoneuroses and its symptoms that he retained the most elements, something which entitles us to the deepest understanding of this "basic language".

Alain Gibeault has observed that these investigations of dreams progressively led Freud to introduce a narrower definition of "symbol". In addition, Gibeault has expressed his astonishment regarding Freud's effort to remove all symbolic activity from dreamwork, because, according to him, the latter determines a set of relationships between the manifest content and the latent content which one can in fact call symbolic: one meaning is substituted for another, which both conceals and expresses it. From this perspective, all the forms of representations, indirect and figurative, of an unconscious desire – dreams, slips of tongue, symptoms, parapraxes, etc. – are symbolic, and dreamwork thus accomplishes a genuine work of *symbolisation* through its distorting effects. It is nevertheless a matter of a particular kind of symbolisation, since in this substitution of representations, the link between the manifest symbol and what is latently symbolised is not evident.[73] That is why Gibeault maintains that dreamwork constitutes genuine work of symbolisation in its two aspects of substituting one representation for another and attempting to connect and master affects.

In speaking, in his way, of the symbolic language of societies which expresses one of the domains of activities of unconscious representation, Freud ultimately connects up with Durkheim's and Mauss' thought. Furthermore, through this field of the symbolic, a connection is made between these two orders of reality, individual and collective, justifying in Freud's mind psychoanalysis' central position between psychopathology and the cultural sciences.

The bobbin game

The bobbin game described by Freud in *Beyond the Pleasure Principle* (1920) in connection with his one-and-a-half-year-old grandson launched the discovery of other exemplary, non-pathological forms of individual symbolisation through its two processes, which, on the one hand, connected two heterogeneous psychical representatives and, on the other, connected an affect to the symbol which would remain floating without it. Let us look at his touching description of it:

> This good little boy ... had an occasional disturbing habit of taking any small objects he could get hold of and throwing them away from him into a corner, under the bed, and so on, so that hunting for his toys and picking them up was often quite a business. As he did this he gave vent to a loud, long-drawn-out "o-o-o-o", accompanied by an expression of interest and satisfaction. His mother and the writer of the present account were

88 Symbols, symbolism and symbolisation

agreed in thinking that this was not a mere interjection but represented the
German word "*fort*" ["gone"]. I eventually realized that it was a game and
that the only use he made of any of his toys was to play "gone" with them.
One day I made an observation which confirmed my view. The child had
a wooden reel with a piece of string tied round it. It never occurred to him
to pull it along the floor behind him, for instance, and play at its being a
carriage. What he did was to hold the reel by the string and very skilfully
throw it over the edge of his curtained cot, so that it disappeared into it, at
the same time uttering his expressive "o-o-o-o". He then pulled the reel
out of the cot again by the string and hailed its reappearance with a joyful
"*da*" ["there"]. This, then, was the complete game – disappearance and
return. As a rule one only witnessed its first act, which was repeated untir-
ingly as a game in itself, though there is no doubt that the greater pleasure
was attached to the second act.[74]

Through this creative activity of a ludic kind, the child was going to try to connect his instinctual excitation triggered by the absence of his mother – a painful
experience undergone passively – therefore to assure mastery of it through his
active attitude marked by "compulsive repetition". The symbolisation of this
game therefore proves to be twofold: on the one hand, there is a substitution of
a representation (the bobbin, which disappears and reappears) for another one
(that of the mother absent in reality, whom the child makes reappear as wished);
on the other hand, there is a linking of unpleasant affects, separation anxiety and
pain, to a representation, that of the bobbin game.

The pleasure acquired also seems to be twofold. Besides the pleasure of master-
ing affects of anxiety and pain reflecting a narcissistic triumph, there is that of the
satisfaction of hostile motions, the mother being transformed in this game into an
object which one can manipulate at will, throw away and make reappear.

Thus, the exploration of this game enabled Freud to identify, notably, links
between symbolisation, sublimation, creativity and elaboration of the loss of
the object, something which would foster the discovery and investigation of an
immense field of individual symbolisations relative to all forms of creative activity, whether ludic or artistic, in particular.

Circumcision: a ritual collective practice

The major stages of any individual's life cycle (birth, puberty, initiation, marriage, death) are marked by "rites of passage" often involving procedures performed on the body (deformations, piercings, extraction or sharpening of teeth,
circumcision, excision of the clitoris and other types of ablation, scarification,
tattooing) that modifying its natural state and are performed in accordance with
rules particular to each society. This *bodily marking* enables a collectivity as a
whole, as well as each one of its members, to express the specific character of
a collective and/or individual identity. Through it, a person manifests his or

Symbols, symbolism and symbolisation **89**

her status and social affiliation. Among the multiple modes of bodily marking, circumcision attracted Freud's interest, especially in *Totem and Taboo* and *Moses and Monotheism*.

This work of bodily marking asserted itself as a form of work of collective symbolisation characteristic of *Kulturarbeit*. In *Totem and Taboo*, he wrote,

> When our [Jewish] children come to hear of ritual circumcision, they equate it with castration. The parallel in social psychology to this reaction by children has not yet been worked out, so far as I am aware. In primaeval times and in primitive races, where circumcision is so frequent, it is performed at the age of initiation into manhood and it is at that age that its significance is to be found; it was only as a secondary development that it was shifted back to the early years of life. It is of very great interest to find that among primitive peoples circumcision is combined with cutting the hair and knocking out teeth or is replaced by them, and that our children, who cannot possibly have any knowledge of this, in fact treat these two operations, in the anxiety with which they react to them, as equivalents of castration.[75]

In *Moses and Monotheism*, Freud presented circumcision as a mark of "consecration" of the Jewish people by Moses, their founder, a visible sign isolating them from foreign peoples[76] that thus became an identifying mark, a source of narcissistic satisfaction. In addition, as a symbolic substitute for castration, it would symbolise this people's submission to their founding father.

> When we hear that Moses made his people holy [p. 30] by introducing the custom of circumcision we now understand the deep meaning of that assertion. Circumcision is the symbolic substitute for the castration which the primal father once inflicted upon his sons in the plenitude of his absolute power, and whoever accepted that symbol was showing by it that he was prepared to submit to the father's will, even if it imposed the most painful sacrifice on him.[77]

In 1980, in *Problématiques II, Castration–Symbolisations*, Laplanche observed that circumcision appeared and developed against the backdrop of a logic of the phallic phase. Unlike Freud, he held that it could not be considered either as a milder offshoot of a mythical castration of prehistorical times or as simply doubling for castration. It stands in a fundamentally and originally ambiguous relationship to castration and to the difference between the sexes, something which is characteristic of any true symbolisation.

Having come to the end of this exploration of symbolism and symbolisation in Freud, Durkheim and Mauss, the time has come to compare what they had to say and the thought underlying it.

Elements for discussion

Symbols

Durkheim developed an objective, substantialist and representative conception of symbols, establishing a univocal relationship between symbols and what is symbolised, unlike Mauss, who, from the time of *A General Theory of Magic*, emptied symbols of all representative content and, through analogy with the linguistic signs, attributed a purely formal, relative dimension to them. Thus, with Mauss symbols no longer connect predetermined terms but signs which are relative entities, the meaning of which pertains to the interplay of their mutual relations within the system they form together.

Looking at the representative dimension of symbols, Durkheim's and Freud's approaches seem to converge there, as well as in terms of the individual relationship between symbol and what is symbolised.

However, we must remember that, in Freud, all forms of representations – figurative and indirect – are symbolic of an unconscious desire – dreams, slips of tongue, symptoms and parapraxes, in particular – and the requirement to connect affects accounts for the specific nature of the symbolisation inherent in unconscious formations and therefore for the concealment of the relationship between symbols and what is symbolised. However, would Durkheim's collective symbols indirectly represent a collective unconscious desire, as the individual formations of the unconscious do? This notion of unconscious desire obviously does not have a place in his terminology.

Furthermore, Freud and Durkheim also meet on common ground when it comes to the conjunction of force and meaning that would constitute every symbolic representation, while Mauss' early reference to the linguistic model would distance him considerably from Durkheim, but also from Freud, both then linked by representation.

Indeed, in Durkheim, collective representations are "forces", and in Freud, individual representations are modalities of psychic expression of the instinct, itself defined as the border concept between the somatic and the psychic.

But, with respect to this, were Durkheim and Freud talking about the same thing when it came to the notion of representation? Let us look at that right now.

In *The Division of Labor in Society* (1893), Durkheim wrote about the notion of representation in the following terms: "a representation is not a simple image of reality, a motionless shadow projected into us by things. It is rather a force that stirs up around us a whole whirlwind of organic and psychological phenomena".[78] And later on, he explained that it was a matter of an effective impulsion, which does not result from the things themselves but from an internal dynamism, that is to say from underlying sentiments and forces, hence its cognitive value which is completely symbolic.

He adapted the notion of collective representation from that of individual representation conceived at the very heart of the relationship between subject and object.

In "Individual and Collective Representations" (1898),[79] he declared that, as the mental life of the individual is composed of individual representations, so collective life is made up of social representations, which he presumes are both comparable to the extent that they undergird the same relationship with their respective substrates.

Thus, the representative life constituted by individual representations has brain matter as its substrate, but this brain matter is not inherent to its intrinsic nature. It is something new. Once these representations exist, they continue to exist on their own and are liable to act directly upon one another, to combine in accordance with their own laws.

However, he laid down that representation can only be defined by the consciousness, and the notion of an unconscious representation seemed to him to be inconceivable. And yet, he considered that representative life extended beyond our present consciousness, and the conception of a psychological memory becomes intelligible: this memory exists, without our having chosen from among the possible manners of conceiving it.

He considered that for its part, society

> has for its substratum the mass of associated individuals. The system which they form by uniting together ... is the base upon which social life is raised. The representations which form the network of social life arise from relations between the individuals thus combined or secondary groups that are between the individual and the total society.[80]

At the same time, they overflow them and preserve their independence. Collective life is thus both dependent and distinct from its substrate.

Consequently, Durkheim maintained that the

> conception of the relationship which unites the social substratum and the social life is at every point analogous to that which undeniably exists between the physiological substratum and the psychic life of individuals. ... The same consequences should then follow on both sides.[81]

What about the notion of representation in Freud?

According to him, representation was what about the object comes to be inscribed in the "mnesic systems" of the subject, something which reflects his particular conception of the memory and of "mnesic trace", which is always inscribed in systems in relationship with other traces (or "signs").

Indeed, in *The Interpretation of Dreams* (1900), Freud discussed the functioning of two distinct systems: a *Pc-Cs* system, which receives the perceptions but does not retain any permanent trace of them, and "unconscious mnesic systems", located behind, where the permanent traces (mnesic traces) of the excitations received are produced. He then established a topographical distinction between

92 Symbols, symbolism and symbolisation

preconscious and unconscious, any given event therefore inscribing itself within these different "mnesic systems".

Right from the beginning, this term designated a sensorial investment visual (of "things", objects) or acoustic (of words and, by extension, of words read), and the *representance* consisted of a process of investment of the mnesic trace in which the representation originated. Freud therefore differentiated between the "representations of things" and the "representations of words", and in accordance with a topographical distinction, the conscious representation includes the representation of the thing, plus the representation of the relevant word, while the unconscious representation is the representation of the thing alone (1915).

These so very different conceptions of the notion of representation obviously reflect specific features proper to each one's epistemological field, themselves conditioned by the nature of the realities explored, which were unconscious intrapsychic–individual for Freud, and the sociocultural and collective for Durkheim.

As for Mauss, while he already referred to the linguistic model and tried to elaborate a theory of signs in *A General Theory of Magic*, it must be remembered that in his 1924 lecture, the notion of symbol became the agency of mediation and of connection between the social and the psychological, between the collective and the individual, something which distanced him all the more from Durkheim but at the same time drew him nearer to Freud. He considered that the social had become a dimension of all human phenomena, like the psychic, and biological, moreover. In addition, he would reintroduce the body alongside the psychic and the social, through instinct and "rhythm", and would associate instinct and symbol. Note that this Maussian "instinct-symbol" pair is found again, in a certain way, in Freud, notably in his understanding of hysterical symptoms bringing him to discover that the human body, erogenous body and instinct are sources of symbolisation.

Symbolism and symbolisation

Durkheim explored the exclusively collective dimension of symbolism, which he situated within the more general framework of collective representations localised within a hypothetical "collective consciousness".

It was a matter of the language of every society which expresses ideas, feelings and images in this way. It constituted both an instrument of intersubjective communication and a factor of communion and social unity. But it was also the way of thinking of every collectivity, enabling it not only to reflect upon itself but also to represent to itself its environment and its relationships with it. Remember that this symbolism is accompanied by what he called "idealism", "creator of reality", something which would correspond to the collective imaginary activity depicted by symbols, the language of the social imaginary. This is the way it is with religious thought in particular. Through this notion of idealism, we find similarities with the Freudian notion of phantasy activity, which would be symbolized in various different forms.

Symbols, symbolism and symbolisation **93**

Moreover, detectable in this field of collective symbolism as thought and elaborated by Durkheim are the two processes of symbolisation discovered by Freud in his clinic of neuroses: on the one hand, that of association between two representations; and, on the other hand, that of the linking of an affect by a representation. Likewise, we identify the role and importance of the object lost in the appearance of a process of collective symbolisation, notably, in the symbolisation of social feelings. Thus, when Durkheim declared that, "in order to express our own ideas to ourselves we need to anchor them in material things that symbolize them",[82] and when social feelings endure through symbols, we find both the link between two representations – symbolised and symbolising – and the representation linking an affect, making its mastery possible. Symbolisation of what no longer exists – the affect of mourning, the pain of loss and of absence – will, consequently, be able to find a material or ideal representation which will link this affect, all the while presentifying the absence, something which Freud objectivised in a remarkable way through his analysis of the bobbin game.

But, contrary to Mauss, Durkheim would hold on to this collective symbolic activity, therefore excluding any possible connection with individual thought. In this Durkheimian conceptualisation, there is definitely a concern with establishing and maintaining a solution of continuity between the social realm and the psychological realm, which he had to establish for reasons of identity and epistemology. It was a matter of founding sociology as a science that was finally emancipated at one and the same time from philosophy, psychology and biology, even though we find in Durkheim a double language – biological and psychological – as well as a biological paradigm, and even also the temptation to make sociology into a "special" psychology, *sui generis*, or a collective psychology, because of the necessary study of collective representations.

For his part, Mauss related symbolism to the symbolic activity of the human mind, whether collective or individual, and fully recognized that symbolic thought is the primary form of human thought, that it underlies all thought. Thus, with this symbolic activity of the mind, there no longer exists, unlike in Durkheim, any split between the social and the individual, but rather transitions, mediations and relationships of interdependence.

In addition, it is no longer a matter of only saying, as his uncle had, that social life would be impossible without symbolism. It was necessary to add that symbolism is just simply *the condition for any group as a group*. Indeed, while Durkheim sought to have symbolism arise from the state of society, responding thus to its needs, Mauss said that it was the appearance of symbolic thought which makes social life both possible and necessary. Consequently, *the symbolic proves to be something unique and functionally necessary to the human world*.

In *De Durkheim à Mauss, l'invention du symbolique*, Tarot rightly considers that this problem of symbolisation seems to provide the true ground for observing the relationships between Durkheim and Mauss and consequently the transition from one to the other. While Durkheim proposed the construction of a

94 Symbols, symbolism and symbolisation

sociological theory of symbolisation, Mauss introduced us to a symbolic theory of society fitting into the framework of the elaboration of an anthropology of the symbolic as a deep orientation, which from that time on he made sociology and anthropology adopt, but also as a project in which he invited specialists of the social and human sciences to participate.

For his part, Freud would tackle the collective dimension of symbolism on the basis of the vast field of the *symbolic*, of which dreams were a part. Considering that the immense majority of dream symbols were sexual symbols, and observing a distinct contrast between the wealth of sexual symbols and the paucity of things symbolised by multiple, quasi-equivalent symbols, he could not refrain from assuming the existence of a particularly close relationship between genuine symbols and sexuality, something to which Durkheim and Mauss would certainly not subscribe!

In addition, through the *symbolic* there appears, according Freud, the possibility of a certain universal language or "basic language" which subjects have at their disposal, beyond the diversity of cultures and languages and which, in certain cases or on certain points, would then permit trans-individual deciphering. He in fact discovered, on the one hand, that this *symbolic* was shared with psychoneuroses, where the most elements were preserved – something which allows us, moreover, the most profound understanding of this "basic language". On the other hand, he found that it actually belonged to the "activity of unconscious representation" of peoples. It was therefore not only individual in nature, but also collective in nature.

There is therefore detectable a major point of convergence between Mauss and Freud with regard to the human foundations of symbolism, something which obviously distanced them from Durkheim.

Mauss held that it was a matter of a production of the "symbolic activity of the mind", whether individual or collective, while Freud called the "activity of unconscious representation" that of individuals or peoples, as agent of individual products such as symptoms and dreams, but also of collective products, myths, legends and other things. Elsewhere, in "A Short Account of Psycho-Analysis" (1924), Freud would talk about the notion of activity of the human mind. Both conferred upon this activity of the human mind – unconscious on the one hand, and symbolic, but also by nature unconscious, on the other – the status and role of mediation, of transition among the three dimensions of all human reality: biological, psychological and social. Relationships of translation and expression would exist among them.

However, by associating neurotic symptoms and repressed sexual content, on the one hand, and dream symbols and essentially sexual content, on the other, and consequently underpinning this "activity of unconscious representation" by desire, Freud radically diverged from Mauss, who principally made reference to the unconscious nature of linguistic facts of a cognitive kind, something which would be amply developed by Lévi-Strauss. And yet, he had written that magic is "the domain of the desire." But it is not there a matter of sexual desire!

Moreover, let me emphasize with Freud the contrast between the paucity of unconscious symbolised things and the wealth of symbols and symbolic thought, a characteristic to which Mauss would subscribe.

In contrast, when Mauss emphasised that social particularities are *arbitrary*, but necessarily functional owing to the constraints of life in a group, and that they result from processes of symbolisation, he was both near to Freud and far from him when the latter dealt with individual symptoms, which in fact proceed from individual symbolisations, therefore, from "non-universal", "individual particularities". However, they are not "arbitrary" but overdetermined, grounded in unconscious phantasies reflecting the infantile lives of subjects. In this respect, Freud probably drew closer to the Durkheimian notion of "idealism", "the creator of reality", relative to an activity of the collective imaginary filled with needs, desires, feelings, expectations, hopes and ideals, but quite obviously devoid of sexual content.

Moreover, writing in *Moses and Monotheism* (1939) about the universality of the symbolic of the language and of the symbolic relation detectable in children and dreams, Freud related them to "thought dispositions", meaning to innate contents representing elements of an *archaic* or *phylogenetic inheritance*. He thus came to affirm that the dreams and neuroses, as well as cultural products – such as the most ancient legends and ancient customs, among other things – would be the "repositories" of the contents of the *archaic inheritance* transmitted from generation to generation. It is quite probable that Mauss and Durkheim would have rejected this notion of archaic inheritance, especially Mauss, who had already opposed the evolutionist thought of his uncle.

Finally, one last reflection. Freud could refute Mauss' statement addressed to psychologists in these words, "Whereas you descry these cases of symbolism only quite rarely, and often within series of abnormal facts, we apprehend great numbers of them all the time and within immense series of normal facts".[83]

Indeed, while Freud brought to light the work on the symbolisation of neurotic symptoms, he also demonstrated in an exemplary fashion that dreams – daily, normal individual products – are another form of symbolic production, which draws both upon the collective *symbolic* and upon the individual work of symbolisation, disguising in this way the latent thoughts bearing, notably, infantile sexual phantasies, just as the ludic activity of children, but also the diverse forms of individual artistic creation, in particular, represent many other normal individual symbolic products.

Having come to the end of my discussion, which above all consisted of identifying some convergences and divergences among Freud, Durkheim and Mauss, I find that it has notably highlighted the radical differences and specific nature of the unconscious intrapsychic-individual, and historical, sociocultural collective realities which determine a thought and an appropriate language building a singular methodology and epistemology. However, involvement of ideological and identity issues can contribute to strengthening these essential differences, something which is obvious in Durkheim, as opposed to Mauss, who was precisely

96 Symbols, symbolism and symbolisation

trying to grasp the *whole person* in three dimensions, but with his methodological tools derived from sociology, as well as from ethnology, historical criticism, linguistics and psychology.

For we are after all dealing with human reality, which is so complex; that is why inevitable convergences exist, something which I have tried to emphasise.

Notes

1 Émile Durkheim, "Introduction to Ethics", in W. S. F., Pickering (ed.), *Durkheim: Essays on Morals and Education*, Abingdon, Routledge, 2009, pp. 77–96. Originally published as "Introduction à la morale," *Revue philosophique* 89, 1920, pp. 79–97.
2 *Op. cit.*, Émile Durkheim, *Division of Labor in Society*, New York NY, The Free Press, 1997 (1983), p. 52.
3 *Ibid.*, pp. 53–56.
4 *Ibid.*, p. 179.
5 *Ibid.*, pp. 57, 82, 101, 177.
6 *Ibid.*, pp. 99–100, 177, 316, 322.
7 *Ibid.*, p. 178.
8 Émile Durkheim, "Définition du fait moral", in *Textes*, vol. 2, Paris, Minuit, 1975 (1893), pp. 257–288, cited here pp. 275–276.
9 *Op. cit.*, Durkheim, *Suicide, a Study in Sociology*, p. 312.
10 *Ibid.*, p. 313.
11 For example, *op. cit.*, Durkheim, *The Elementary Forms of Religious Life*, p. 171.
12 *Ibid.*
13 *Ibid.*, p. 172.
14 *Ibid.*, p. 173.
15 *Ibid.*
16 *Ibid.*, p. 173, n. 1.
17 *Ibid.* p. 173.
18 *Ibid.*, pp. 174, 240.
19 Émile Durkheim, "The Problem of Religion and the Duality of Human Nature", in *Knowledge and Society: Studies in the Sociology of Culture, Past and Present*, vol. 5, Henrika Kuklick and Elizabeth Long (eds.), Greenwich CT, JAI Press, 1984 (1913), pp. 1–11, 15–20, 22–31, 39–41.
20 *Op. cit.*, Durkheim, *The Elementary Forms of Religious Life*, p. 175.
21 *Ibid.*, pp. 176–77.
22 Camille Tarot, *De Durkheim à Mauss, l'invention du symbolique*, Paris, La découverte, 1999.
23 *Op. cit.*, Karsenti, p. 210.
24 *Op. cit.*, Durkheim, *The Elementary Forms of Religious Life*, p. 175.
25 *Ibid.*
26 *Op. cit.*, Karsenti, p. 212.
27 *Op. cit.*, Durkheim, *The Elementary Forms of Religious Life*, p. 173.
28 *Op. cit.*, *De Durkheim à Mauss, l'invention du symbolique*.
29 *Op. cit.*, Mauss, *A General Theory of Magic*, pp. 119–120. I have replaced the word "representations" with the word "forces", which appears in this English translation because Mauss used the Durkheimian term "*forces*" in the original text, which is important for understanding Durkheim's influence on his thought during this period of his work.
30 *Ibid.*, p. 132.
31 *Ibid.*, p. 148.
32 *Ibid.*, p. 149.
33 *Ibid.*, p. 156.

Symbols, symbolism and symbolisation **97**

34 *Ibid.*, p. 178.
35 Marcel Mauss, "Real and Practical Relations between Psychology and Sociology", in *Sociology and Psychology, Essays Marcel Mauss*, London, Routledge and Kegan Paul, 1979, pp. 1–33.
36 Mauss, *The Gift: The Form and Reason for Exchange in Archaic Societies*, p. 5.
37 *Ibid.*, p. 70.
38 *Ibid.*, p. 33.
39 *Ibid.*, p. 46.
40 *Ibid.*, p 76.
41 *Op. cit.*, Karsenti.
42 Claude Lévi-Strauss, *Introduction to the Work of Marcel Mauss*, Abingdon, Routledge, 1987 (1950), pp. 63, 64.
43 *Op. cit.*, Karsenti, p. 249.
44 *Op. cit.*, Tarot, *Le symbolique et le sacré*, p. 271.
45 *Op. cit.*, Tarot, *De Durkheim à Mauss, l'invention du symbolique.*
46 Marcel Mauss, "Civilizational Forms", in *Rethinking Civilizational Analysis*, S. Arjomand and E. Tiryakian (eds.), London, Sage Publications Ltd., 2004 (1929), pp. 21–29. Cited here is p. 28.
47 *Op. cit.*, Karsenti, p. 306.
48 Sigmund Freud, *Studies on Hysteria*. S.E. 2, London, Hogarth, 1895.
49 *Ibid.*, p. 144.
50 *Ibid.*, p. 174.
51 *Ibid.*, p. 176.
52 *Ibid.*, p. 153.
53 *Ibid.*, p. 180.
54 *Ibid.*, p. 176.
55 *Ibid.*, pp. 180–181.
56 Sigmund Freud, "Fragment of an Analysis of a Case of Hysteria", S.E. 7, 3, 1905, pp. 46–47.
57 Alain Gibeault, *Les chemins de la symbolisation*, Paris, Presses Universitaires de France, 2010.
58 Sigmund Freud, "Papers on Metapsychology", in *On the History of the Psycho-Analytic Movement, Papers on Metapsychology and Other Works*, S.E., 14, London, Hogarth, pp. 109–215.
59 Sigmund Freud, *Introductory Lectures on Psycho-Analysis* (Parts I and II), S.E. 15, London, Hogarth, 1915–1916, p. 152.
60 *Op. cit.*, Stekel.
61 Sigmund Freud, *The Interpretation of Dreams*, S.E., 4, London, Hogarth, 1900a, p. xxvii.
62 Jean Laplanche, *Problématiques II, Castration-Symbolisations*, Paris, Presses Universitaires de France, 1980, p. 282.
63 *Op. cit.*, Freud, "Symbolism in Dreams, Lecture X", *Introductory Lectures on Psycho-Analysis* (Parts I and II), S.E., 15, 1915–1916, p. 150.
64 *Op. cit.*, Freud, *The Interpretation of Dreams*, S.E., 5, 1900a, pp. 358–359.
65 *Op. cit.*, Freud, "Symbolism in Dreams, Lecture X", *Introductory Lectures on Psycho-Analysis* (Parts I and II), S.E., 15, 1915–1916, p. 152.
66 *Ibid.*, p. 165.
67 *Ibid.*, p. 168.
68 Sigmund Freud, *The Interpretation of Dreams*, S.E., 5, 1900a, London, Hogarth, p. 352.
69 *Op. cit.*, Freud, "Symbolism in Dreams, Lecture X", *Introductory Lectures on Psycho-Analysis* (Parts I and II), S.E., 15, 1915–1916, p. 166.
70 *Ibid.*, pp. 158–159.
71 *Op. cit.*, Freud, *The Interpretation of Dreams*, S.E., 5, 1900a, p. 351.
72 Sigmund Freud, *Moses and Monotheism*, S.E., 23, London, Hogarth, 1939, pp. 98–99.

98 Symbols, symbolism and symbolisation

73 *Op. cit.*, Gibeault, p. 58.
74 Sigmund Freud, *Beyond the Pleasure Principle*, S.E., 18, London, Hogarth, 1920, pp. 14–15.
75 Sigmund Freud, *Totem and Taboo*, S.E., 13, London, Hogarth, 1912–1913, p. 153, n. 1.
76 *Op. cit.*, Freud, *Moses and Monotheism*, p. 30.
77 *Ibid.*, p. 122.
78 *Op. cit.*, Durkheim, *Division of Labor in Society*, p. 75.
79 Émile Durkheim, "Individual and Collective Representations", in *Sociology and Philosophy*, edited by Émile Durkheim, London, Cohen and West, 1953, pp. 1–34. Reprinted Abingdon, Routledge, 2010.
80 *Ibid.*, p. 24.
81 *Ibid.*, p. 25.
82 *Op. cit.*, Durkheim, *The Elementary Forms of Religious Life*, p. 173.
83 Cited, *op. cit.*, Lévi-Strauss, *Introduction to the Work of Marcel Mauss*, pp. 10–11.

BY WAY OF CONCLUSION

Our exploration of this vast, complex field of symbolism and symbolisation through the revolutionary conceptions of Freud, Durkheim and Mauss raises some inevitable and necessary questions, one of which forces itself upon us: what became of them, or what was their fate within the human and social sciences, particularly in France, during the second half of the 20th century?

After Freud and his disciples, symbolism and the processes of individual symbolisation were explored and studied by the post-Freudian, notably in the field of the psychoanalysis of children with Melanie Klein, Hanna Segal and Donald Woods Winnicott, in particular, and in that of psychoses. However, those working on the subject do not seem to have pursed their investigation of the collective dimension of symbolism which had been quite developed by the pioneering generation.

So, among these post-Freudian psychoanalysts, it is to Lacan that I shall turn, for reasons I shall give later on.

What about the legacy of Durkheim's and Mauss' ideas?

Let us look at their legacy for the two fields of French anthropology and sociology with Lévi-Strauss and his structuralist revolution; Françoise Héritier and Maurice Godelier, two of his colleagues at the Laboratory of Social Anthropology of the Collège de France; and then Pierre Bourdieu, who was an ethnologist before becoming a sociologist.

To begin with, let me explain some aspects of the historical context.

Between the two world wars, certain academics developed an image of a moralising, conservative, dogmatic Durkheimism, something which brought about his rejection by the young generation of both anthropologists and sociologists, among whom Lévi-Strauss played a determinant role in this regard. This trend prevailed after 1945. Moreover, historians of the human sciences have observed that a fundamental change took place, at least in France, between 1945 and 1950.

100 By way of conclusion

It was a matter of formulating a new paradigm, that of the "symbolic whole", connected with the "structuralist revolution" effected by Lévi-Strauss, which took place at the same time in different ways in several disciplines – sociology, anthropology, psychoanalysis, linguistics and philosophy, for example – or which spread from one to the other. Thus, whether it is a matter of language, concepts, methods, problems, choice of subjects or research orientations, one can detect both a pre- and a post–Lévi-Straussian structuralism – which was above all a vast intellectual and scientific movement – and the project to not only re-found the human sciences definitively but also to unify them, something which pursues the undertaking initiated by Mauss through his conception of the *whole person* and of the mind's symbolic activity, collective as well as individual, in particular.

As Tarot maintained in *Le symbolique et le sacré*, structuralism and its legacy managed to crush Durkheim's influence. The process effected a schism and imposed a taboo. Structuralism definitely originated in the French school of sociology, but divided its legacy by choosing the brilliant precursor Mauss as opposed to the dogmatic, obsolete founder Durkheim.[1] From then on, starting with Mauss, social anthropology would deal with societies as symbolic systems, interested in configurations, looking for structures and demonstrating the consistency of the phenomena it would interpret.

Moreover, I would like to stress again with Tarot that it was no accident that structuralism took hold from 1945 to 1950, in the aftermath of the most terrible episode of European history, but began in the region of the world the least affected by it, America. In structuralism, everything is an implicit reaction to this terrible historical violence. It goes about it in a displaced, euphemised form, as if the page had been turned all the same, perhaps so that at least science might not founder.[2]

Lévi-Strauss and his structuralist revolution

Structuralism would therefore strive to realise the Maussian project of unifying the human and social sciences through the symbolic produced by the human mind and its unconscious structure, something which would ultimately lead Lévi-Strauss to make the unconscious their unifying agent.

His *Introduction to the Work of Marcel Mauss*,[3] first published in *Sociologie et anthropologie* in 1950 – the very year Mauss died – is considered by specialists as marking the birth of structuralism or as being its founding text.

There Lévi-Strauss emphasised the modernity of Mauss' thought to the point of making it structuralist (Tarot). Commenting on the paper about the relations between psychology and sociology, he took up the definition of social life as being "a world of symbolic relationships"[4] and maintained that

> [i]t is natural for society to express itself symbolically in its customs and its institutions; normal modes of individual behaviour are, on the contrary, never *symbolic in themselves:* they are elements out of which a symbolic system, which can only be collective, builds itself.[5]

Later on, Lévi-Strauss presented his famous definition of culture as a

> combination of symbolic systems headed by language, the matrimonial rules, the economic relations, art, science and religion. All the systems seek to express certain aspects of physical reality and social reality, and even more, to express the links that the relations that those two types of reality have with each other and those that occur among the symbolic systems themselves.[6]

In addition, according to him,

> [i]ndividual psychical processes do not reflect the group; even less do they pre-form the group [...]. That *complementarity* of individual psychical structure and social structure is the basis of the fruitful collaboration, called for by Mauss, which has come to pass between ethnology and psychology. But that collaboration will only remain valid if ethnology continues to claim a leading place for the description and the objective analysis of customs and institutions for the psychological study in depth of their subjective aspects can consolidate the leading position of objective analysis, but can never relegate it to the background.[7]

Lévi-Strauss discusses a subordination of the psychological to the sociological which Mauss actually brought to light.

Indeed, as Tarot emphasises in *Le symbolique et le sacré*, Mauss was not a structuralist, and, what is more, he was more than an "ancestor" of structuralism. This founding text would also lay the foundations for an interpretation of the history of ideas which wrested Mauss away from Durkheimism, and symbolism from the science of religions, to make it into the object of the sciences of language. Indeed, according to Tarot, the whole importance of the *Introduction to the Work of Marcel Mauss* lies in substituting the symbolic for the sacred of the French school of sociology. In addition, Lévi-Strauss clearly identified the social with language, that is to say, with a symbolic system, drawing inspiration, in so doing, from Mauss' *A General Theory of Magic* (1902–1903).[8]

Finally divorced from his uncle, Mauss became the guarantor of the Lévi-Straussian conception of symbolic thought. This interpretation was also accompanied by a change in the hierarchy of sciences. While sociology was considered as the organizer of social sciences, in keeping with Durkheim's initial project, linguistics, especially phonology, represented notably by Troubetzkoy and Jakobson, became the model of reference and was given the credit for having realised the "epistemological break" evoked during the 1950s and 1960s. It is to be noted that this change had already been initiated by Mauss himself, establishing linguistics but not phonology as the new model of the social sciences, affording them access to a scientificity limited up until then.

His creation

Structuralism attempted to reach the forms alone. Meaning was no longer in the object, its essence or its substance but in the interplay of its relations with other objects. Thus, the *structuralist act* empties elements of their content in order to grasp them in their interrelations with other elements, interrelations which confer meaning upon them. All the systems of meaning (myths, kinship, art, language, the savage mind, for example) find their common foundation in the symbolic nature of the activity of the human mind, the particularity of structural analysis being to reveal the nature of this activity. For Lévi-Strauss, structure is primary, that is to say that the set of relations and principles governing symbolic systems are fundamental data of social reality and belong to the structural unconscious. He reduced social life to the conditions of symbolic thought, as it were, the foundation of which is constituted by "the unconscious structure of the human mind", hence the symbolic origin of society. Consequently, if the ethnologist's job is to explore the unconscious elements of social life – in the sense defined by Mauss, but also by the American anthropologist Franz Boas, who both refer to linguistic facts, and not by Freud – then "ethnology is first of all psychology", as Lévi-Strauss wrote in *The Savage Mind*,[9] but a non-affective, cognitive psychology, where the body, the instincts and the affects have no place and imaginary activity is excluded. In this respect, he takes leave, of not only the "idealism, creator of reality" and the power of affects claimed by Durkheim, but also the importance Mauss accorded to the body, to instincts and affects representing then one of the dimensions of the *whole person*.

Symbolic and unconscious

In "The Effectiveness of Symbols" (1949),[10] Lévi-Strauss engaged in a radical critique of the definition of the Freudian unconscious, creating out of it a new definition, structuralist in nature, that constituted one of the theoretical foundations of his anthropology, which would particularly inspire Lacan, in his "return to Freud". There he defined the unconscious as a totality constituted by formal laws, with the result that his own logic is a formal logic. In fact, from this perspective the unconscious produces a symbolism whose expressions are detectable on multiple levels which appear as just so many structures, that is to say as just so many formal spaces. He wrote:

> The unconscious ceases to be the ineffable refuge of individual peculiarities, the repository of a unique history which makes each of us an irreplaceable being. It is reducible to a function – the symbolic function, which no doubt is specifically human, and which is carried out according to the same laws among all men, and actually corresponds to the aggregate of these laws.
>
> If this view is correct, it will probably be necessary to re-establish a more marked distinction between the unconscious and the preconscious than has been customary in psychology. For the preconscious, as a reservoir of recollections and images amassed in the course of a lifetime, is merely an aspect

of memory. [...] The unconscious, on the other hand, is always empty – or, more accurately, it is as alien to mental images as is the stomach to the foods which pass through it. As the organ of a specific function, the unconscious merely imposes structural laws upon inarticulated elements which originate elsewhere – instincts, emotions, representations, and memories.[11]

This is why Lévi-Strauss could in turn announce the disappearance of the dividing line between the collective mind and the individual mind, as Mauss had done in his 1924 lecture, but it would only be realised on the unconscious level, something which Freud had already formulated and claimed well before Mauss. Nevertheless, this pre-eminence of the symbolic function, unconscious in nature, conditioning a formal conceptualisation of social phenomena and favoured by the structural interpretation, could correspond to an adulteration of the Maussian methodology based, in particular, upon a complex, eclectic, concrete approach to social phenomena.

Françoise Héritier and the body as the founding substrate of the original categories of symbolic thought: the identical and the different

Françoise Héritier was first interested in the vast field of kinship, particularly exploring the semi-complex systems that she also encountered in the Samo of sub-Saharan Africa, thus extending the work initiated by her mentor Lévi-Strauss on the elementary structures of kinship. With this as her starting point, her questions about incest and its prohibition led her to investigate the symbolic dimension, from then on opening up for her the realm of the symbolic and thus connecting up with her illustrious predecessors there. She established a fruitful link between what she designated by the new notion of *symbolic work* and its "universal biological substrate", namely the body, the difference between the sexes, its organs, its fluids (sperm, menstrual blood, milk) and their circulation and the bodily functions, while pursuing one of the research orientations initiated by Mauss, something which would also bring her closer, in a certain way, to the Freudian spirit, considering the sexed body as a source of symbolisation.

Let us therefore look at some elaborations that she proposes of the reflections initiated by Durkheim and Mauss, then pursued by Lévi-Strauss.

She considers that, inserted into the natural environment, a place of observation of the difference between the sexes and of the procreative relationship, the body is the first object of human reflection and constitutes the *founding substrate of original categories of symbolic thought, those of identical and different.* Difference is expressed in opposites or binary categories, the first pair of which, male/female, acts as a paradigm relative to the others and is subject to hierarchical ordering (male > female). From this universal given would follow the creation of social institutions and systems of representation and of thought, that is to say of an "ideological body" and therefore of a symbolic order. Symbolic discourse

104 By way of conclusion

would therefore be built upon a system of dualistic pairs accounting for the order of the world, the social order, for example: hot/cold, dry/wet, sun/moon, upper/lower, light/heavy, hard/soft ... So, among the Samo, the main dualistic category contrasts hot and cold and their corollaries dry and wet and acts as a mechanism explaining institutions and events.

What about the notion of *symbolic work*, or "symbolic manipulation of the real and its constants" out of the same universal biological material that it is a matter of "recreating"?

In *Masculin/Feminin. La pensée de la différence* (1996), Héritier considers that kinship systems are a notably good example of *symbolic work*. Indeed, for her, a kinship system is not the expression of the pure biological fact of reproduction but necessarily takes into account basic biological data.[12] It is a matter of the existence of two sexes which must come together in order to procreate, something which brings about a succession of generations, the natural order of which cannot be reversed. An order of succession of births within the same generation brings the recognition of older and younger siblings. All three of these natural relationships, Héritier explains, express difference within male/female, parent/child and eldest/youngest relationships. It is this banal material, in its universal simplicity, that the *symbolic work of kinship* manipulates in all times and all places by effecting series of derivations among these three orders of facts, from which the terminological systems, the rules of filiation, the rules of marriage and those of residence have resulted.[13] Moreover, she shows us the existence of a relationship of inequality not based on biology, finding expression, notably, in all the terminological systems in which it is possible to transpose the men/women and/or eldest/youngest relationships in the parents/children relationship, something which would not be conceivable for the women/men or youngest/eldest relationships, women and youngest then being in the dominant position. It would be a matter of a proof, according to her, that every kinship system is a symbolic manipulation of the real, a logic of the social.[14]

These original categories of the identical and the different seem to me to belong to the cognitive realm, referring to an anthropology of the symbolic, of an essentially cognitivist nature and orientation, thus continuing in the spirit of Lévi-Strauss' endeavours. Found there, notably, is the binary categorisation, the universality of formal laws, to the detriment of the variability of symbolic contents and their latent unconscious meanings. Nevertheless, by considering the body as the founding substrate of the original categories of symbolic thought, she actually re-establishes a connection with Mauss, then broken by Lévi-Strauss.

Maurice Godelier's critique

Confronted with the structuralist omnipotence of the symbolic, Godelier meant to defend the primacy of the imaginary which necessarily combines with the symbolic and the diverse forms of symbolisation. He in fact considers that the never really defined, polysemic collective imaginary activity is the great victim sacrificed by structuralist thought. However, it proves just as productive of collective representations, objects of beliefs, as it is constructive of sociocultural reality through its symbolic manifestations in institutions and ritual practices, in particular.

Let us look along with him at the exemplary matter of incest and its prohibition.

While Héritier became involved in an investigation of their fundamentally symbolic dimension and discovered a logic of the identical and the different at work, Godelier includes incest among the "misuses of sex" – along with necrophilia and zoophilia, for example – variously repressed and punished depending on the society and the times because of the danger they represent for the reproduction of society and the balance of the universe; he also partly shares his colleague's analysis in terms of symbolic logic of the identical and the different. Nevertheless, he explains that incest is but a particular case, among others, of the universal subordination of sexuality to the reproduction of society. He distances himself from Héritier by introducing the essential contribution of the collective imaginary. He in fact considers that since the social order is not only a moral order and a sexual order but also a cosmic order, most of the time the reasons invoked for these sexual prohibitions are at once social, moral and religious ("cosmic"), that is to say, both *real* and *imaginary*. These imaginary explanations, objects of shared collective beliefs, are interpretations of social reality and therefore pertain to an "ideal" (*idéel*) reality existing only in the mind and through the collective mind, but they also produce social reality through their crystallisation in institutions and their staging and enactment in symbolic practices and rituals, validating and legitimising, in return, those collective representations.[15] However, Godelier considers that there is something arbitrary in this collective imaginary production.

Thus, with this resurrection of the imaginary, collective in this instance, Godelier is reviving the so invaluable Durkheimian notion of "idealism, creator of reality" presented in *The Elementary Forms of Religious Life* (1912),[16] which can only function with symbolism conferring multiple forms upon it. Moreover, through sexuality and the body, after the fashion of his colleague Héritier, he distanced himself from Lévi-Strauss to rejoin Mauss and the multi-dimensionality of the *whole person*.

Pierre Bourdieu, symbolic power and violence

Heir to Lévi-Straussian structuralism but also thinking in the wake of the thought of Marx and Weber, Bourdieu approached the symbolic from the standpoint of the problem of power and developed a "structuralo-Marxism" polarised by a theory of domination.

He complemented the Marxist analysis of the relationships of force that are part of the social structure with one of the effectiveness of symbols themselves, inspired by Lévi-Strauss, in order to discover properly symbolic mechanisms of the power said to be *symbolic*. Nevertheless, Bourdieu differed from Lévi-Strauss,

106 By way of conclusion

according to Erwan Dianteill, both by paying heightened attention to incorporated dispositions which imperfectly generate systematic symbolic practices[17] and by reintroducing the violence banished from the social order by the structuralist reduction to the "symbolic whole".

According to Bourdieu, power is split into two parts, visible and non-visible, from the start. Visible power is grounded in force and overt conflict, while the other, invisible power hides everywhere and always presents itself in disguised form. It is a matter of the power called *symbolic*, based on ignorance of victim's condition as a victim, which would be at the very basis of the system of domination. The symbolic violence it implies would therefore only impose domination by concealing the fact of its domination.

Inseparable from symbolic power, Bourdieu therefore strove to think through this *symbolic* violence. Thus, as violence, symbolic violence is first of all class violence, having its source in real groups in conflict, but, as symbolic, it is internalised by the habitus and, therefore, systematised and unrecognised.

Moreover, this invisible power is first mediated by symbolic systems (language, art and religion, for example) as multifunctional "structuring structures". They are in fact instruments of knowledge, of ordering the world, but also of communication, transmitting meaning and serving to produce common meaning. Finally, they fulfil a social function of integration.

Thus, with the reintroduction of the violence and power called symbolic, not only at the heart of the social, of its structures and functioning, but also with their internalisation by the habitus, Bourdieu exhumed the dimension of violence of social relationships. It is to be recalled that it was discovered and formulated by Mauss in his *The Gift* (1924)[18] with respect to the North American Indian practice of *potlatch* and destructive struggles for prestige, something which would be the object of massive denial on the part of Lévi-Strauss and structuralists.

But let us stop here in order to close our journey with Lacan.

Lacan and the symbolic function

Curiously, Freud's reflections on symbolism and symbolisation did not seem to have had any direct impact on Lacanian thought. However, according to the sociologist and psychoanalyst Markos Zafiropoulos in his book *Lacan and Lévi-Strauss, or Freud's Return, 1951–1957* (2003),[19] it was Lévi-Strauss' work, through both his notions and concepts and his structural method, which infiltrated Lacan's thinking, in his reinterpretation of Freud's "great clinical cases" as well as in his conceptual work during the 1950s and thus guided his "return to Freud", something which would have an impact on the international and French psychoanalytical field.

First of all, the Lévi-Straussian conception of the unconscious, notably that expounded in "The Effectiveness of Symbols" (1949), was for Lacan a particularly invaluable tool for interpreting Freud's writings, leading him to elaborate a new model of exploration and interpretation of the unconscious, its processes and formations. He appropriated the notion of symbolic function, which he would situate at the very origin of the structuration of the "subject of the unconscious", where the image of the body and the symbolic dimension are well connected. In so doing, he promoted *this universal symbolic function within psychoanalysis, something which had never happened in its history.*

In his "return to Freud", he reintroduced the function of death and of the dead father, a cornerstone of the symbolic function, into analytical experience. In addition, he likened the function of speech and its laws to the symbolic function. Moreover, he established the OEdipus complex as a "simple" symbolic situation present in modernity and conferred upon the superego a symbolic status having roots in symbolic exchanges having even preceded the subject's birth. Thus, as symbolic function, the superego now comes from the Other of the culture; it is a symbolic formation, a language formation which determines the child's situation with regard to the symbolic system before his or her birth. This symbolic organisation is the subject's Other, from which his or her life proceeds and to which he or she remains indebted. This notion of debt was, by the way, borrowed from *The Gift* by Mauss.

This major place of Lévi-Straussian thought in the construction of this new theoretical system created by Lacan during the 1950s was expressed in exemplary fashion in 1953 in the "Rome Discourse",[20] a discourse on the theoretical foundations of the new Société Française de Psychanalyse, which he had just joined after leaving the Société Psychanalytique de Paris. Lacan set forth there his fundamental project of revealing the primacy of the symbolic structures and of language in the object of the Freudian discovery, the unconscious. This revealing had in fact to go by way of the "scientific restoration" of Freudian concepts, for which he wanted to show a certain correspondence with anthropological concepts. In this way, by integrating the contemporary findings of anthropology into its theoretical corpus, in this case structural anthropology, psychoanalysis could find its place, and a harmonious one, among the human sciences. In this regard, there was, for Lacan, a community of essential objects, that of the symbolic structures which organise the unconscious and make psychoanalysis and those disciplines interdependent. He indicated, for example, the lead taken by Lévi-Strauss' work in the exploration itself of the unconscious.

Let us remember that this symbolic function, originating in the work of the English neuropsychologist Henry Head, was borrowed by Mauss to designate the mechanism of production of meaning at the heart of social life. It would therefore be retrieved by Lévi-Strauss to characterise the unconscious and then henceforth put into the foundations of the theoretical system elaborated by Lacan.

I shall bring our journey to an end by specifying that there were other avenues of utilisation, development and transformation of these revolutionary conceptions, the processes, purposes, and issues of which for the most part remain ideological in nature, that is to say pervaded by unconscious representations, beliefs and affects, in spite of justifications of a scientific nature. One finds this

108 By way of conclusion

throughout the whole history of ideas, as was amply demonstrated in my earlier book, *The Oedipus Complex, Focus of the Psychoanalysis-Anthropology Debate* (2009).[21] That is necessarily part of the *humanness* of any scientific elaboration.

Finally, one last consideration. If this theme of symbolism and symbolisation – through the symbolic activity of the mind, of the unconscious structure defended by Mauss and then Lévi-Strauss, and the "activity of unconscious representation" defined by Freud – promised to become a juncture-mediation between the collective and individual fields, the present-day scientific reality is in fact quite nuanced. However, if it was meant to contribute to eliminating the split and then to unifying the human sciences, we can but note its failure, in spite of Lévi-Strauss' structuralist experiment. Indeed, to varying degrees and according to variable modalities, the gap has even widened through unconscious resistance on the part of the diverse specialists impelled once again by ideological concerns and feelings of identity endangerment which discredit genuinely scientific interests.

Thus, no matter what the object of knowledge and the multidimensional (historical, sociocultural or institutional, in particular) framework into which it necessarily fits, the history of the sciences and ideas regularly shows us a conflict between its two structural poles – scientific and ideological – which will ever constitute a major obstacle to both its investigation and its future.

Notes

1 *Op. cit.*, Tarot, *Le symbolique et le sacré*, p. 48.
2 *Ibid.*, p. 672.
3 Claude Lévi-Strauss, *Introduction to the Work of Marcel Mauss*, Abingdon, Routledge, 1987 (1950).
4 *Ibid.*, p. 10.
5 *Ibid.*, p. 12.
6 *Ibid.*, p. 16.
7 *Ibid.*, pp. 22–23.
8 Marcel Mauss, *A General Theory of Magic*, London, Routledge, 1972 (1902).
9 Claude Lévi-Strauss, *The Savage Mind*, Chicago, University of Chicago Press, 1966 (1962), p. 131.
10 Anthologized in Claude Lévi-Strauss, *Structural Anthropology*, New York, Basic Books, rev. ed. 1974 (1949), pp. 186–205.
11 *Ibid.*, pp. 202–203.
12 Françoise Héritier, *Masculin/Feminin. La pensée de la différence*, Paris, Odile Jacob, 1996, p. 56.
13 *Ibid.*, p. 57.
14 *Ibid.*, p. 67.
15 Maurice Godelier, *The Metamorphoses of Kinship*, London, Verso, 2011 (2004).
16 Émile Durkheim, *The Elementary Forms of Religious Life*, Oxford, Oxford University Press, 2001 (1912).
17 Erwan Dianteill, "Pierre Bourdieu et la religion. Synthèse critique d'une synthèse critique", *Archives de sociologie des religions*, 118, 2002, p. 7.
18 Marcel Mauss, *The Gift: The Form and Reason for Exchange in Archaic Societies*, London, Routledge, 1990 (1925).

19 Markos Zafiropoulos, *Lacan and Lévi-Strauss, or Freud's Return, 1951–1957*, London, Karnac, 2010 (2003).
20 Jacques Lacan. "Function and Field of Speech and Language in Psychoanalysis", *Ecrits: a Selection*, London, Tavistock/Routledge, 1977 (1949), pp. 9–32.
21 Eric Smadja, *The Oedipus Complex, Focus of the Psychoanalysis-Anthropology Debate*, London, Routledge, 2017 (2009).

BIBLIOGRAPHY

Abraham, Karl, "Dreams and Myths: A Study in Folk-Psychology", in *Clinical Papers and Essays on Psycho-Analysis*, London, The Hogarth Press and the Institute of Psychoanalysis, 1955, pp. 153–210.

Anzieu, Didier, *Freud's Self-Analysis*, London, Hogarth Press and the Institute of Psycho-Analysis, 1986 (1959).

Assoun, Paul-Laurent, *Freud et les Sciences Sociales*. Paris: Armand Colin, 1993.

Assoun, Paul-Laurent, *Introduction à l'épistémologie Freudienne*, Paris, Payot, 1981.

Cassirer, Ernst, *Philosophy of Symbolic Forms*, New Haven CT, Yale University Press, 1955–1957 (1923–1929).

Creuzer, Friedrich, *Symbolik und Mythologie der alten Völker, Besonders der Griechen*, Leipzig, Karl Wilhelm Leske, 1810–1812.

Dianteill, Erwan, "Pierre Bourdieu et la religion. Synthèse critique d'une synthèse critique", *Archives de sociologie des Religions*, 118, 2002.

Durkheim, Émile, "Apports de la sociologie à la psychologie et à la philosophie", in his *Textes*, vol. 1, Paris, Minuit, 1975 (1909), pp. 184–188.

Durkheim, Émile, "Définition du fait moral", in his *Textes*, vol. 2, Paris, Minuit, 1975 (1893), pp. 257–288.

Durkheim, Émile, *Division of Labor in Society*, New York NY, The Free Press, 1997 (1893).

Durkheim, Émile, "Individual and Collective Representations", in *Sociology and Philosophy*, Émile Durkheim (ed.), London, Cohen and West, 1953, pp. 1–34. Reprinted London, Routledge, 2010.

Durkheim, Émile, "Introduction to Ethics", in W. S. F. Pickering (ed.), *Durkheim: Essays on Morals and Education*, London, Routledge, 2009, pp. 77–96. Originally published as "Introduction à la morale," *Revue Philosophique* 89, 1920, pp. 79–97.

Durkheim, Émile, "La Science positive de la morale en Allemagne", *Revue Philosophique* 24, 1887, pp. 33–58, 113–142, 275–284.

Durkheim, Émile, "Leçons sur la morale". Notes taken by G. Davy of lectures on "La Morale" that Durkheim gave at the Sorbonne, probably from 1908–1909 his lecture–course, translated in Steven Lukes' *Émile Durkheim: An Intellectual Biography* (thesis

112 Bibliography

presented for the degree of Doctor of Philosophy, deposited at Bodleian Library in Oxford), vol. 2, 1968, pp. 248–260.

Durkheim, Émile, "Lo stato attuale degli studi sociologici in Francia", *La Riforma sociale* 3, 1895, pp. 607–22, 691–707.

Durkheim, Émile, "M. Aslan, *La Morale de Guyau*", *Revue de Métaphysique et de Morale* 14, supplément juillet: 14. Examination of thesis, 1906.

Durkheim, Émile, "Remarque sur la méthode en sociologie", in his *Textes*, vol. 1, Paris, Minuit, 1975 (1906), pp. 58–61.

Durkheim, Émile, "Remarques sur le problème de l'individu et de la société", in his *Textes*, vol. 1, Paris, Minuit, 1975 (1893), pp. 56–57.

Durkheim, Émile, *The Elementary Forms of Religious Life*, Oxford, Oxford University Press, 2001 (1912).

Durkheim, Émile, "The Problem of Religion and the Duality of Human Nature", in *Knowledge and Society: Studies in the Sociology of Culture, Past and Present*, vol. 5, Henrika Kuklick and Elizabeth Long (eds.), Greenwich CT, JAI Press, 1984 (1913), pp. 1–11, 15–20, 22–31, 39–41.

Durkheim, Émile, "The Psychological Conception of Society (1901)", anthologised in his *The Rules of Sociological Method*, New York NY, The Free Press, 1982 (1895).

Durkheim, Émile, *The Rules of Sociological Method*, New York NY, The Free Press, 1982 (1895).

Durkheim, Émile, "Sociology", in *Émile Durkheim,1858–1917: A Collection of Essays, with Translations and a Bibliography*, Kurt Wolff (ed.), Columbus OH, Ohio State University Press, 1960 (1900).

Durkheim, Émile, "Sociology and Its Scientific Field," in Kurt Wolff (ed.), *Émile Durkheim, 1858–1917: A Collection of Essays, with Translations and a Bibliography*. Columbus OH, Ohio State University Press, 1960 (1900), pp. 354–375 and as "The Realm of Sociology as a Science", *Social Forces* 59, 4, 1981, pp. 1054–1070.

Durkheim, Émile, "Sociology in France in the Nineteenth Century", in *Émile Durkheim on Morality and Society, Selected Writings*, in Robert Bellah (ed.), Chicago, The University of Chicago Press, 1973 (1900), pp. 6–10.

Durkheim, Émile, *Suicide, a Study in Sociology*, New York NY, The Free Press, 1951 (1897).

Fournier, Marcel, *Émile Durkheim: A Biography*, Cambridge UK, Polity Press, 2013.

Fournier, Marcel, *Marcel Mauss: A Biography*, Princeton NJ, Princeton University Press, 2006 (1994).

Freud, Sigmund, *Beyond the Pleasure Principle*, S.E., 18, London, Hogarth, 1920.

Freud, Sigmund, *Fragment of an Analysis of a Case of Hysteria*, S.E. 7, 3, London, Hogarth, 1905.

Freud, Sigmund, *The Interpretation of Dreams*, S.E., 4, London, Hogarth, 1900a.

Freud, Sigmund, *The Interpretation of Dreams*, S.E., 5, London, Hogarth, 1900a.

Freud, Sigmund, *Introductory Lectures on Psycho-Analysis* (Parts I and II), S.E., 15, London, Hogarth, 1915–1916.

Freud, Sigmund, *Moses and Monotheism*, S.E., 23, London, Hogarth, 1939.

Freud, Sigmund, "Papers on Metapsychology", in *On the History of the Psycho-Analytic Movement, Papers on Metapsychology and Other Works*, S.E., 14, London, Hogarth, 1915, pp. 109–215.

Freud, Sigmund, *"Psycho-Analysis" and "Theory of Libido"*, S.E., 18, London, Hogarth, 1923.

Freud, Sigmund, *Psycho-Analysis*, S.E., 20, London, Hogarth, (1926f).

Freud, Sigmund, *Studies on Hysteria*, S.E., 2, London, Hogarth, 1895.

Bibliography 113

Freud, Sigmund, "Symbolism in Dreams, Lecture X", in *Introductory Lectures on Psycho-Analysis* (Parts I and II), S.E., 15, London, Hogarth, 1915–1916.

Freud, Sigmund, *Totem and Taboo*, S.E., 13, London, Hogarth, 1912–1913.

Fustel de Coulanges, Numa Denis *The Ancient City*, Baltimore MD, Johns Hopkins Press, 1980 (1864).

Gibeault, Alain, *Les chemins de la symbolisation*, Paris, Presses Universitaires de France, 2010.

Godelier, Maurice, *The Metamorphoses of Kinship*, London, Verso, 2011 (2004).

Héritier, Françoise, *Masculin/Feminin. La pensée de la différence*, Paris, Odile Jacob, 1996.

Hubert, Henri, *The Rise of the Celts* and *The Greatness and Decline of the Celts*, first published in English in a single volume entitled *The History of the Celtic People*, London, Kegan Paul, Trench, Trubner, 1934.

Jones, Ernest, *On the Nightmare*, London, The Hogarth Press, 1931.

Jones, Ernest, *Sigmund Freud, Life and Work. Vol 1: The Young Freud 1856–1900, Vol 2: The Years of Maturity 1901–1919. Vol 3: The Last Phase 1919–1939*, London, Hogarth Press, 1953–1957.

Jones, Ernest, "The Madonna's Conception through the Ear: A Contribution to the Relationship between Aesthetics and Religion", in Ernest Jones (ed.), *Essays in Applied Psycho-Analysis*, vol. 2, London, Hogarth Press, 1951, pp. 266–357.

Jones, Ernest, "The Symbolic Significance of Salt in Folklore and Superstition", in *Salt and the Alchemical Soul*, Stanton Marlan (ed.), Woodstock CT, Spring Publications, 1995, pp. 47–100.

Jones, Ernest, "The Theory of Symbolism", *British Journal of Psychology* 9, 1916, 181–239.

Jung, Carl Gustav, *Psychology of the Unconscious: A Study of the Transformations and Symbolisms of the Libido, a Contribution to the History of the Evolution of Thought*, London, Kegan Paul Trench Trubner, 1916 (1912). Revised in 1952 as *Symbols of Transformation*, published in his Collected Works, vol. 5, Princeton NY, Princeton University Press.

Karsenti, Bruno, *L'homme total: Sociologie, Anthropologie et Philosophie Chez Marcel Mauss*, Paris, Presses Universitaires de France, 1997.

Lacan, Jacques, "Function and Field of Speech and Language in Psychoanalysis", in *Ecrits: a selection*, London, Tavistock/Routledge, 1977 (1949), pp. 9–32.

Lacan, Jacques, *Les Écrits Techniques de Freud*, Paris, Seuil, 1975.

Laplanche, Jean, *Problématiques II, Castration-Symbolisations*, Paris, Presses Universitaires de France, 1980.

Lévi-Strauss, Claude, *Introduction to the Work of Marcel Mauss*, Abingdon, Routledge, 1987 (1950).

Lévi-Strauss, Claude, *Structural Anthropology*, New York, Basic Books, rev. ed. 1974 (1949), pp. 186–205.

Lévi-Strauss, Claude, *The Elementary Structures of Kinship*, Boston MA, Beacon Press, 1969 (1949).

Lévi-Strauss, Claude, *The Savage Mind*, Chicago, University of Chicago Press, 1966 (1962).

Mauss, Marcel, *A General Theory of Magic*, London, Routledge, 1972 (1902).

Mauss, Marcel, "Civilizational Forms", in *Rethinking Civilizational Analysis*, S. Arjomand and E. Tiryakian (eds.), London, Sage Publications Ltd., 2004 (1929), pp. 21–29.

Mauss, Marcel, "Divisions et proportions des divisions de la sociologie", *L'Année sociologique*, n.s. 2, 1927, reprinted in his *Œuvres*, vol. 3, Paris, Minuit, 1969.

Mauss, Marcel, "L'École anthropologique anglaise et la théorie de la religion selon Jevons", *Œuvres*, vol. 1, 1968.

114 Bibliography

Mauss, Marcel, *Manuel d'ethnographie*, Denise Paulme (ed.), Paris, Payot & Rivages, 2002 (1926).

Mauss, Marcel, "Rapports réels et pratiques de la psychologie and de la sociologie", in Mauss, *Sociologie et anthropologie*, 3rd ed., Paris, Presses Universitaires de France, 1924, pp. 281–310.

Mauss, Marcel, "Real and Practical Relations between Psychology and Sociology", in *Sociology and Psychology, Essays Marcel Mauss*, London, Routledge and Kegan Paul, 1979, pp. 1–33.

Mauss, Marcel, *The Gift: The Form and Reason for Exchange in Archaic Societies*, London, Routledge, 1990 (1925).

Ogden, C. K. and I. A. Richards, *The Meaning of Meaning: A Study of the Influence of Language upon Thought and of the Science of Symbolism*, 10th ed. With supplementary essays by Bronislaw Malinowski and F. G. Crookshank, London, Routledge & Kegan Paul, 1949 (1923).

Rank, Otto, *Die Lohengrinsage. Ein Beitrag zu ihrer Motivgestaltung und Deutung*, Leipzig, Deuticke, 1911.

Rank, Otto, *The Incest Theme in Literature and Legend*, Baltimore MD, Johns Hopkins Press, 1991 (1912).

Rank, Otto, *The Myth of the Birth of the Hero*, Baltimore MD, Johns Hopkins, 2004 (1909).

Rank, Otto and Hanns Sachs, "The Significance of Psychoanalysis for the Humanities", *The American Imago, a Psychoanalytic Journal for the Arts and Sciences* 22, 1964 (1913), pp. 6–133.

Ribot, Théodule, *English Psychology*, New York, D. Appleton, 1874 (1870).

Ribot, Théodule, *German Psychology To-Day, The Empirical School*, New York, Charles Scribner's Sons, 1886 (1870).

Ribot, Théodule, *The Psychology of the Emotions*, London, Walter Scott Ltd., 1897.

Schorske, Carl E., *Fin-De-Siecle Vienna. Politics and Culture*. New York, Vintage Books, 1981.

Smadja, Eric, *The Oedipus Complex, Focus of the Psychoanalysis-Anthropology Debate*, London, Routledge, 2017 (2009).

Spencer, Herbert, *The Study of Sociology*, New York, D. Appleton & Co., 1873.

Stekel, Wilhelm, *Sex and Dreams: The Language of Dreams*, Boston, The Gorham Press, 1922 (1911).

Tarot, Camille, *De Durkheim à Mauss, l'invention du symbolique*, Paris, La découverte, 1999.

Tarot, Camille, *Le symbolique et le sacré: théories de la religion*, Paris, La découverte, 2008.

Wolff, Kurt (ed.), *Émile Durkheim, 1858–1917: A Collection of Essays, with Translations and a Bibliography*, Columbus OH, Ohio State University Press, 1960 (1900).

Zafiropoulos, Markos *Lacan and Lévi-Strauss, or Freud's Return, 1951–1957*, London, Karnac, 2010 (2003).

INDEX

academic group, sociology 30
academic socialism 33
activity of unconscious representation 108
adolescence: Durkheim, Émile 23–24;
  Freud, Sigmund 7; Mauss, Marcel 42
agnostic foundation, psychoanalysis 20
Alcan, Félix 27
"Analysis terminable and interminable"
  (Freud) 16
The Ancient City (Durkheim) 24
Annales sociologiques 48
L'Année sociologique 27, 44, 47
antagonism 84
anthropology 51
L'Antisémite 25
Anzieu, Didier 11, 17
aphasia 2
archaic inheritance 86–87, 95
Archives d'anthropologie criminelle 29
associative determinism 79
Assoun, Paul-Laurent 19–21
astasia-abasia 79–80
Autobiography (Freud) 15

basic language 86–87
battle of the methods 19
Bernard, Claude 31
Bernays, Martha 8
Beyond the Pleasure Principle (Freud) 15, 87
Bleuler, Eugen 13
bobbin game 87–88
bodies 103
bodily marking 88–89

Le Bon, Gustave 31
Bouglé, Célestin 27
Bourdieu, Pierre 105–106
Boutroux, Émile 24
Brentano, Franz 7
Breuer, Josef 9–10
Broca, Paul 29
Brücke, Ernst 7, 20

circumcision 88–89
Civilization and Its Discontents (Freud) 15
"Civilization Forms" (Mauss) 77
clan flags 62
cocaine 8
collective affective states 68
collective consciousness 71, 92
collective existence 67
collective feeling 65
collective forces 69
collective imaginary production 105
collective life 62
collective mind 71
collective psychology 52
collective realities 37
collective representations 37, 64–65,
  67, 90
communication, symbols 71
communion 66
compulsive repetition 88
Comte, Auguste 24, 32
"Constructions in analysis" (Freud) 16
conversion 80
"creator of reality" 67–68, 92

116 Index

Creuzer, Friedrich 2
criminologist group, sociology 29
cults, rituals 64
culture: as defined by Lévi-Strauss 101;
immergence of psychoanalysis 17

Darwin, Charles 31
De Durkheim à Mauss; l'invention du symbolique (Tarot) 93
death 107
delirium, religion 63–64
descriptive sociology 46
Le Devenir social (Mauss) 43
Dianteill, Erwan 106
Die Traumdeutung (Freud) 11
Dilthey, Wilhelm 19
The Division of Labor in Society (Durkheim) 24, 26, 90
"Divisions et proportions des divisions en sociologie" (1927) (Mauss) 50
domain of desire 75
dream-interpretation 84
dreams 21, 83–87
Dreyfus, Louise 25
Durkheim, Émile 1, 2; collective representations and symbols 65; *The Division of Labor in Society* 90
Durkheimian symbol 65–66; *Elementary Forms of Religious Life* 62–63; French school of sociology 28–39; idealism 67–68; *L'Année sociologique* 27; Law as symbol of social solidarity (1893) 60–62; legacy of 47–48; religion 62–64; *Suicide* 62; symbolisation 67; symbolism 67, 92; symbols 66–67, 90–91; teaching experiences in Bordeaux 25–26
Durkheimian method 37–39
Durkheimian symbol 65–66
Durkheimism 31–34; Mauss, Marcel 50–57; pluralism 51–53; social facts 35–37, 38, 50–51; society 34–35

École d'anthropologie de Paris 29
École normale supérieure, Durkheim 24–25
economic animals (homo oeconomicus) 74
"The Effectiveness of Symbols" (Lévi-Strauss) 102, 106
The Ego and the Id (Freud) 15
Elementary Forms of Religious Life (Durkheim) 28, 62–63
epistemological break 101
epistemological foundations of psychoanalysis 20

Espinas, Alfred 30
Essai sur les variations saisonnières des sociétés Eskimos (Mauss and Beauchat) 45, 55
ethnographical and anthropological group, sociology 29
ethnography 46
ethnologists 102
ethnology 34, 102; French ethnology 53–54; Maussian ethnology 55–56; exchange in archaic societies 72–74
exchanges–gifts 73
Exner, Sigmund 7

false connections 79
family; Durkheim, Émile 23; Freud, Sigmund 6; Mauss, Marcel 42;
Fechner, Gustav 21
Fechnero-Helmhotzian model 20
Fédération des Jeunesses Socialistes Révolutionnaires 45
Fliess, Wilhelm 10
Fouillée, Alfred 24, 30
Fournier, Marcel 25–27, 42
France, sociology 28–30
Frazer, James 34
French ethnology 53–54
Freud, Sigmund 2, 3, 78; *Beyond the Pleasure Principle* 87; bobbin game 87–88; circumcision 88–89; *The Interpretation of Dreams* 91; *Introductory Lectures on Psycho-Analysis* 83; *Moses and Monotheism* 86, 89, 95; *Papers on Metapsychology* 82; psychoanalysis 16–22; representations 91–92; self-analysis 18; *Studies on Hysteria* 79; symbolic production, symptoms 79–83; symbolism of dreams 83–87; symbols 90–91; *Totem and Taboo* 89; *Freud et les sciences sociales* (Assoun) 19, 21
"Freud Society" 13
The Future of an Illusion (Freud) 15

Geisteswissenschaften 19
general phenomena 55
A General Theory of Magic (Mauss and Hubert) 45, 68–70, 74
Gibeault, Alain 82, 87
The Gift: The Form and Reason for Exchange in Archaic Societies (Mauss) 47, 72–74, 77–78
gifts 77–78
Godelier, Maurice, critique of structuralism 104–105
Group Psychology and the Analysis of the Ego (Freud) 15
Gurvitch, Georges 57

Index

Haeckel, Ernst 21
Hall, Stanley 13
Head, Henry 2, 76, 107
Herbart, Johann Friedrich 20
Herbartian model 20
Héritier, Françoise 103–104
Herr, Lucien 25
homo duplex 56
Hubert, Henri 44, 45, 48
L'Humanité 45
hypnosis 9–10
hysteria 10
hysteria of conversion 82
hysterical symbolisation 81

ideal reality 105
idealism 67–68, 92; religion 63–64
If Moses Was an Egyptian (Freud) 16
image-symbol 3–4
Imago (Freud) 14
incest 105
indirect representation 83
"Individual and Collective
    Representations" (Durkheim) 91
individual incarnations 36
individual representations 90
individual symbolisation 84
instinct 71; Mauss, Marcel 77
instinct-symbol 92
Institut d'ethnologie de Paris 47, 53–54
institution 36
interest 74
The Interpretation of Dreams (Freud) 11, 18,
    21, 84, 91
Introduction à l'épistémologie freudienne
    (Assoun) 19
*Introduction à l'étude de la médecine
    expérimentale* (Bernard) 31
Introduction to the Work of Marcel Mauss
    (Lévi-Strauss) 100
Introductory Lectures on Psycho-Analysis
    (Freud) 14–15, 22, 83
invisible power 106
Irma's injection (Freud) 11
Isidor, Mélanie 27

Jackson, Henry 2
Jaurès, Jean 45
Jones, Ernest 14–16
Jung, Carl Gustav 13, 14

Kahane, Max 12
Karsenti, Bruno 1, 2, 52, 65–67,
    74–75, 77–78
kinships 104

Lacan, Jacques, symbolic
    function 106–108
Lacassagne, Alexandre 29
Laplanche, Jean 84, 89
Law as symbol of social solidarity (1893)
    (Durkheim) 60–62
law of causality 32
Le Play, Frédéric 30
Lectures (Freud) 15
Leenhardt, Maurice 57
Letourneau, Charles 29
Lévi, Sylvain 43–44
Lévi-Strauss, Claude 54, 57, 75, 76, 100,
    107; "The Effectiveness of Symbols"
    102, 106; structuralism 100–102;
    symbolic and unconscious 102–104
"The Libido Theory" (Freud) 16
linguistics 101

magic 68–70; symbols 74–75
Malinowski, Bronislaw 73
mana 69–70, 75
Manuel d'ethnographie (Paulme) 54–55
Marillier, Léon 44
Masculin/Feminin. La pensée de la différence
    (Héritier) 104
material props 62
Mauss, Marcel 1, 2, 26, 46, 101;
    ethnology 55–56; French ethnology
    53–54; *A General Theory of Magic*
    68–70, 74; *The Gift: The Form and
    Reason for Exchange in Archaic Societies*
    72–74, 77–78; legacy of Durkheim
    47–48; politics 47; "Real and Practical
    Relations between Psychology and
    Sociology" 70–71, 75–77; symbolism
    77–78, 93; symbols 90–92; teaching
    based on Manuel d'ethnographie
    54–55; transforming-developing
    Durkheimian sociology 50–57; whole
    person 56–57
Maussian ethnology 55–56
Maussian symbols 74–75
mechanical solidarity 61
metapsychology 20
methodological eclecticism 51–53
milieu 69
mnesic symbols 79
mnesic systems 92
modality 56
monistic foundation, psychoanalysis 20
morality, Durkheim 61–62
Moses, an Egyptian (Freud) 16
Moses and Monotheism (Freud) 16, 86,
    89, 95

118 Index

Le Mouvement Socialiste 45
Musée de l'Homme 54, 57

nationalities 47
natural reality 32
Naturwissenschaften 19
negative cult 64
notion of instinct 71

objectification 74
objective psychology 33
OEdipus complex 18, 107
On Aphasia (Freud) 10
"On the History of the Psycho-Analytic
    Movement" (Freud) 14
organic solidarity 61
Other 107
An Outline of Psycho-Analysis (Freud) 16

Papers on Metapsychology (Freud) 82
phenomena of totality 56, 72
phobias 82–83
physicalist foundation, psychoanalysis 20
physiology 55
pluralism 51–53
politics, Mauss, Marcel 47
positive cult 64
potlatch 73
power 105–106
preconscious 102–103
"The Problem of Nationality" (Mauss) 47
Problematiques II, Castration-Symbolisations
    (Laplanche) 89
process of individualisation 36
"La prohibition de l'inceste et ses origines"
    (Durkheim) 27
Project for a Scientific Psychology (Freud) 11
proliferations 77
"Psycho-Analysis" (Freud) 16
psychoanalysis 14; Freud, Sigmund 16–22
psychoanalytical method 10
psychological naturalism 33

The Question of Lay Analysis (Freud) 15

Radcliffe-Brown, Alfred Reginald 46
Rank, Otto 3
"Real and Practical Relations between
    Psychology and Sociology" (Mauss)
    70–71, 75–77
reality, idealism 67–68
Les règles de la méthode sociologique 26
Reik, Theodor 15
Reitler, Rudolf 12

relationship of association 79
relationship of translation 52
relationships, symbolic relationships 84
religion: as defined by Durkheim 62–64;
    rituals 64
Renouvier, Charles 24
representance 92
representations 20; Freud, Sigmund
    91–92; sociology 36–37
"Return to Freud" (Lucan) 107
Réville, Albert 45
rites of passage 88
rituals, religion 64
Riviere, Joan 15
"Rome Discourse" (Lacan) 107
The Rules of Sociological Method
    (Durkheim) 31, 34–35, 37

Sachs, Hanns 3
Schaeffle, Albert 33
Scherner, Karl Albert 83
Schorske, Carl E. 17
Schreber, Senatspräsident 86
La Science sociale contemporaine (Fouillée) 30
The Second International Congress of
    Psychoanalysis 13
self-analysis, Freud 18
Seligman, Charles Gabriel 46
semantic functions 75
sex, incest 105
sexes 104
sexual phantasy 82
SFIO (socialist republicans and the
    socialists) 53
signification 74–75
signs 75
simple symbolisation 80
Social Change (Mauss) 43
social facts 35–37, 38, 50–51, 72
social language 65
social life 65, 67, 100
social morphology 37, 38, 55
social particularities 77
social phenomenon 36, 50, 77
social physiology 32, 37
social reality 105
social solidarity 60–62
social things 38
social whole 50
Société d'anthropologie de Paris 29
Société d'economie sociale (Le Play) 30
Les sociétés animales (Espinas) 30
society 34–35
sociological method 51

Index **119**

sociology: benefits for psychology 71–72; conception of 27; Durkheimian method 37–39; Durkheimian revolution 31–34; in France 28–30; social facts 35–37; society 34–35
"Sociology and Its Scientific Field" (Durkheim) 32
socio-psychical 36
Sorbonne, Durkheim 27–28
sources of symbolism 2–4
Spencer, Herbert 31
split consciousness 80
Stekel, Wilhelm 12
structuralism 100; critique by Godelier 104–105; Lévi-Strauss, Claude 100–102
structuralist act 102
structuralist revolution, Lévi-Strauss 100
Studies on Hysteria (Freud) 10, 18, 79
The Study of Sociology 31
Suicide (Durkheim) 26, 32, 62
symbolic 94; Bourdieu, Pierre 105–106; dreams 83–87; power and violence 105–106; unconscious and 102–104
symbolic activity of the mind 76
symbolic determinism 79
symbolic expression 2
symbolic function 2, 76, 103; Lacan, Jacques 106–108
symbolic production, symptoms 79–83
symbolic relationships 84
symbolic thought 70, 76
symbolic unity 2
symbolic work 103–104
symbolisation 92–95; bobbin game 87–88; dreams 87; Durkheim, Émile 67; Mauss, Marcel 77; "Real and Practical Relations between Psychology and Sociology" (Mauss) 76; symptoms 80–83
symbolising conversion 83
symbolism 62, 66, 77, 92–95; circumcision 88–89; dreams 83–87; Durkheim, Émile 67; Mauss, Marcel 77–78; "Real and Practical Relations between Psychology and Sociology" (Mauss) 75; as social language 65; sources of 2–4

"Symbolism in Dreams" (Freud) 22
symbols 62, 71, 90–91; collective representations and 65; communication 71; Durkheimian symbol 65–66; *A General Theory of Magic* (Mauss and Hubert) 74–75; mnesic symbols 79; tools of social communication 66–67
symptoms 78; symbolic production 79–83; symbolisation 80–83
system of total services 73
systematic idealisation 64

Tarde, Gabriel 29–30
Tarot, Camille 3, 31, 35, 39, 52, 56, 67, 68, 76, 78, 100
thanatomania 71–72
theories of realities-symbols 3
theory of hysteria 10
theory of libido 21
Three Essays on the Theory of Sexuality (Freud) 13
tools of social communication, symbols 66–67
totem 62–63, 65
Totem and Taboo (Freud) 14, 89
totemic principle 63
totemism 63
translation 72
typical dreams 84
typical symbolic 84

unconscious 102–104, 108

value judgments 70
"Vienna Psychoanalytic Society" 12
violence, symbolic power and 105–106
visible power 106
von Fleischl-Marxow, Ernst 7
von Helmholtz, Hermann 21
von Schmoller, Gustav 33

Wagner, Adolf 33
"Wednesday Psychological Society" 12
whole person 56–57, 100, 102

Zafiropoulos, Markos 106

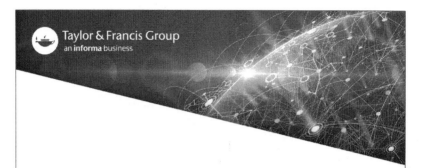